MURDER IN PARADISE

A SERIOUS WARNING TO THE UNITED STATES

& THE ADVENTIST CHURCH

BY NIC SAMOJLUK, PH.D.

****

IT'S NOT TOO LATE TO RESTORE

THE UNBORN'S RIGHT TO LIFE

IF WE WERE ABLE TO ABOLISH SLAVERY

WE CAN ABOLISH THE ABORTION GENOCIDE!

Nic Samojluk holds an MA from *La Sierra College* (now LSU) and a Ph.D. from *Andrew Jackson University*. He is the author of *"From Pro-life to Pro-choice: The Dramatic Shift in Seventh-day Adventists' Attitudes Towards Abortion,"[1]* and of many articles connected with the abortion issue.[2]

---

[1]
http://www.lulu.com/shop/search.ep?type=&keyWords=Nic+Samojluk&sitesearch=lulu.com&q=&x=18&y=15

[2] http://adventlife.wordpress.com; http://advindicate.com/articles/3008; Adventist Today, Vol.15, issue 1, 18.

How to Order Additional Copies of this Book

To order additional copies of this book for your friends and your pastor, click on the link listed at the foot of this page.[3]

How to Order Copies of my Original Book dealing with Abortion

To order copies of my book, *"From Pro-life to Pro-choice: The Dramatic Shift in Seventh-day Adventists Towards Abortion,"* click on the link provided at the bottom of this page.

Pro-life Promotion Fund

If you received a copy of this book as a gift, it was probably paid from a special fund created for said purpose. You are invited to help replenish this fund by giving a donation of any amount to the author. This will allow him to send copies of the book to other influential individuals like you. The author has invested a small fortune for the creation of this book, which means that you can benefit from this research at a tiny cost of what it took to produce it. You can contribute online by clicking on **http://adventlife.wordpress.com** .

Copyright Notice

All rights reserved. No portion of this book can be reproduced without the written permission of its author, except for brief quotations in critical reviews or articles. Most of the illustrations included in this book were harvested from the Internet and quite often bear only a tangential connection with the specific items being presented.

2014 Nic Samojluk. All rights reserved.

ISBN: 978-1-312-15101-7

---

[3] http://www.lulu.com/shop/search.ep?type=&keyWords=Nic+Samojluk&sitesearch=lulu.com&q=&x=18&y=15

 I dedicate this book exclusively to Marta, a loving and Christian woman who stole my heart the first time I met her in the city of La Plata, Argentina, and who has stood by my side through sunshine, rain, and storm since 1957; the year we pledged to each other before the Lord.

This is a sequel to the first book I published entitled *"From Pro-life to Pro-choice: The Dramatic Shift in Seventh-day Attitudes Toward Abortion,"* a book that, according to the opinion of a leading retired Adventist professor, should be read by every Adventist in the world.

This book contains the best from its predecessor and from what I have published since 1994, the year I decided to speak on behalf of those who cannot do it on their own defense. You will discover that some fundamental facts and concepts are repeated throughout its pages for the sake of emphasis.

IF YOU HAVE NO INTEREST IN READING THIS BOOK, OR IF YOU WILL NOT READ IT AGAIN, DO NOT LET IT GATHER DUST—GIVE IT TO SOMEBODY ELSE! LET THE BOOK FULFILL ITS SACRED MISSION!

CONTENTS

INTRODUCTION

The Verdict of History

How will history judge our nation and our Adventist Church? How will future generations judge us? We condemn past generations for tolerating slavery, war, and genocide. History will ever repudiate Nazi atrocities during World War II, but it will reserve its harshest judgment for our present generation because, while past generations killed in war, we kill in peace time.

Former generations killed preferable adults, we target our mass destruction on the unborn; they killed mainly on a retaliatory basis, we kill without provocation; they killed mostly enemies, we annihilate our own children; they killed to protect their national or tribal security, we wage war on totally innocent, defenseless creatures generated in the majority of cases by a deliberate choice of their often irresponsible, sexually careless and promiscuous parents.

We in America condemn the murderous activity of Stalin, who killed millions of his own people; and Hitler, who exterminated six million Jews. How does this compare with the 56 million innocent human beings we annihilated so far since 1973 before they had a chance to take their first breath? Hitler killed his victims and incinerated them inside the gas chambers; we burn them with chemicals inside the sacred chamber God created for their protection.

We strongly condemn the Catholic Inquisition during the Middle Ages for killing thousands of innocent human beings, yet we remain silent and have even profited from the modern genocide of the unborn. We claim to have a message of hope for the world, and we have labeled our nation as a *"shining city on a hill"* yet we offer no hope for the unborn for whom Jesus Christ also died as evidenced by his concern for *"the least of these."*

5

 We Adventists have championed the health cause with our stop smoking program in order to add five years to those addicted to tobacco products, yet we forget that by saving the life of the unborn we can add 80 years or more to their lives instead of merely five.

We have claimed to be members of those who keep God's Commandments, yet we have led the way for the legalization of abortion in our country. Bear in mind that we started offering elective abortions back in 1970—three years before abortion was legalized in the U.S. mainland.

Please, help me understand this! I have written to numerous Adventist publications and to the General Conference, and all I get is: *"This is a controversial issue," "Our church does not have a pro-life program," "Read our "Guidelines on Abortion.""* Aren't issues like Sabbath observance and smoking controversial as well?

Did our Adventist pioneers stay away from issues like temperance and slavery that were highly controversial? Why can't we say, *"Read the Bible,"* or *"Read the Sixth Commandment,"* which forbids murder, instead of telling us to read the *"Guidelines on Abortion"* which were designed to neutralize and void God's dictum against the shedding of innocent blood?

 Our sin against heaven is great, but our Savior is greater! If we repent of our sin, God will gladly pardon us for deviating from the narrow way. But we must, like King Josiah of old, renew our covenant with God and remove the image of Moloch from God's Holy Temple where the Israelite worshippers burned their own children in honor of that most cruel pagan deity. If we refuse to do this, how will we be able to stand firm when our faith will be severely tested under penalty of death?

We failed in Germany half a century ago, we failed in Rwanda more recently, and we failed in 1970 when we started profiting from the slaughter of the unborn. Isn't it time for us to right what is wrong and choose life instead of death if we are planning to stand one day firm for duty like the compass is to the North Pole,?[4]

---

[4] Deut. 30:19; Is.1:18.

New International Version
This day I call the heavens and the earth as witnesses against you that I have set before you life and death, blessings and curses. Now choose life, so that you and your children may live.

New International Version
"Come now, let us settle the matter," says the LORD. "Though your sins are like scarlet, they shall be as white as snow; though they are red as crimson, they shall be like wool.

Murder in the Cathedral

When T.S. Eliot wrote his *"Murder in the Cathedral"* drama following the assasination of Archbishop Thomas Becket in the Canterbury Cathedral in 1170, the impact of his work resonated throughout Europe because you do not expect killings to take place in the sacred precints of a place of worship.

Likewise, the U.S Supreme Court decision to legalize the genocide of millions of unborn children took the world by surprise because the United States has been considered by the entire world as the bastion of freedom and

the most desirable place to live on planet earth. In fact, President Ronald Reagan described our country as *"a shinging city on a hill."* How could such a shining city on a hill allow an open season for the killing of millions of innocent human beings whose only sin was to wait for the right to see the light of day. When the right to be born is destroyed, all other rights and freedoms loose their full meaning for the victims!

Similarly, the Adventist Church decision to profit from abortion back in 1970 took the religious communinity by surprise rsulting in moral revulsion because Adventists had claimed a high regard for the sacredness of the Ten Commandments, one of which forbids the killing of innocent human beings. Adventism was the less likely place for a compromise over the sanctity of God's Law. Since the Adventist Church had stood firm in defense of the sacredness of the Sabbath, people expected the leaders of Adventism to stand firm on the sacred righ to life!

Is Murder the Best Choice of Words?

 Someone may wonder whether *"murder"* might not be the best word to describe the transformation that took place in the United States and Adventism four decades ago. Should I have chosen a less offensive term like *"pregnancy interruption," "termination of pregnancy,"* or *"therapeutic abortion"?* The answer is *"no,"* because murder is defined as the intentional and malicious killing of an innocent human being.

Of course, a person could argue that the unborn is not a human being. Science would deny such an assertion and it confirms that human life begins at the moment of conception. That point in time marks the beginning of human growth. This can be verified by consulting any biology textbook.

Some anti-life individuals believe that the unborn is not a human being in the first trimester of pregnancy. Is such a claim credible? As we look at the pictures of first trimester aborted babies,[5] we see human hands, human feet, and a human head and torso. What kind of animal possesses those characteristics? We conclude that the unborn is definitely a human being regardless of its size and place of residence.

The definition for murder cited above requires that the victim must be free of moral guilt. You probably agree with me that the unborn qualifies! It would be hard to imagine a more innocent human being than the unborn.

I conclude, therefore, that the term Murder is a proper word to describe the action of the U.S. Supreme Court in 1973 and that of the Adventist Church in 1970 when the Adventist Church allowed our Castle Memorial Hospital in Hawaii to offer abortions on demand with impunity[6]

---

[5] http://www.priestsforlife.org/resources/photosbyage/index4.htm

Is Paradise a fit Symbol for the U.S. & the Remnant Church?

Someone may wonder about the choice of paradise as a symbol for the U.S. and the Adventist denomination. Well, paradise is probably the less likely place for a murder to take place, and due to the unambiguous defense of the validity and permanence of the Decalogue by the Adventist community of faith, Adventism was the less likely place for a compromise with evil over the killing of innocent human beings for the sake of filthy profit, especially in the case of abortions on demand or elective abortions.

 The Adventist Church is probably the only denomination still defending the validity and permanence of the Ten Rules for moral behavior inscribed on two tablets of stone by God with his own hands. This is still true in theory at least, although we have negated this in practice. Officially, at least, we still teach that God's Decalogue is in force and will remain in force till the end of time. We believe in the sanctity of Sabbath, the day of rest chosen by the Lord for us, and in our *"Guidelines on Abortion"* we clearly state **"Abortions for reasons of birth control, gender selection, or convenience are not condoned by the Church."**[7]

 How do we justify then teaching one thing and acting in opposition to what we say we believe? The short answer is profit. When the State of Hawaii legalized abortion in 1970, the non-Adventist physician staff at our Castle Memorial Hospital [CMH] demanded the right to offer elective abortions to their patients, and the church caved in for fear of loosing revenue. The fear of God was replaced with the fear of men.

The long answer is found in a book authored by Vance Ferrel entitled *"The Broken Blueprint."* And we should not confuse elective abortions with the so-called *"therapeutic"* kind. What the CMH physicians were fighting for

---

[6]George Gainer, "The Wisdom of Solomon?" Spectrum 19/4 (May 1989): 38-46; "Abortion: History of Adventist Guidelines" Ministry (Aug. 1991): 11-17.
[7]http://www.adventist.org/information/official-statements/guidelines/article/go/0/abortion/6/

was abortions on demand, since said medical institution was already providing abortions in the therapeutic category.

This new policy spread to at least five other additional medical institutions,[8] and one of those was our Washington Adventist Hospital, which was later on described by a General Conference officer as a *"an abortion mill."*[9] George Gainer relates the following anecdote that illustrates this: A pastor decided to take his pregnant wife to our WAH for her maternity care.

No sooner they were in the presence of the hospital OBGN physician, the doctor asked: "Are you planning to keep the baby?" Think about this: What is the alternative of keeping the baby? The man got up and said to his wife: *"Honey, let's go. I think that we are in the wrong hospital."*

Is Our Moral Fall Serious?

Some readers may wonder whether our departure from a *"thus said the Lord"* really serious. Does preoccupation with the killing of unborn children perhaps a sign of a false guilt?

In order to answer this question we would probably do well to bring to mind the experience of King Saul. He received a clear mandate from heaven to destroy the nation of Amalek including the animals.

He carried his mission with unusual success, but he decided to slightly deviate from the instruction given to him through Samuel, God's prophet.

He saved the best of the animals with the excuse that he would use them as sacrificial offerings in God's honor. The problem is that is not what he was instructed to do. When Samuel reprimanded him, the following exchange took place:[10]

---

[8] Gerald R. Winslow, "Abortion Policies in Adventist Hospitals" Specttum 19/4 (May 1989): 47-50.

[9] Teresa & Arthur Beem, "Why we left" Former Adventist Fellowship Online (18 Nov. 2002).http://www.formeradventist.com/stories/teresaarthurbeem.html

[10] 1 Sam. 15:20-22

New International Version
"But I did obey the LORD," Saul said. "I went on the mission the LORD assigned me. I completely destroyed the Amalekites and brought back Agag their king. The soldiers took sheep and cattle from the plunder, the best of what was devoted to God, in order to sacrifice them to the LORD your God at Gilgal."

Can the Adventist Church Fail?

Given this serious moral detour from the right path, someone may ask: Is it possible for the Adventist Church to fail in her mission to the world and be rejected by heaven? Don't we have a large number of prophetic predictions describing the triumph of God's special people? Isn't our victory secure and guaranteed by said promises? The answer is yes, the Lord did predict such an outcome; nevertheless, we need to remember that God's promises and threatening are contingent on our behavior. Notice the promise the Lord made to King David and Solomon. Said promise was contingent on their faithfulness to him:[11]

"As for you, if you walk before me faithfully as David your father did, and do all I command, and observe my decrees and laws, I will establish your royal throne, as I covenanted with David your father when I said, 'You shall never fail to have a successor to rule over Israel. But if you turn away and forsake the decrees and commands I have given you and go off to serve other gods and worship them, then I will uproot Israel from my land, which I have given them, and will reject this temple I have consecrated for my Name. I will make it a byword and an object of ridicule among all peoples. This temple will become a heap of rubble."

---

[11] 2 Chron. 7:17-21.

And we need to bear in mind what happened to Priest Eli and his family. The Lord had promised that Eli's descendants would remain as priests forever, but when he failed to discipline his two sons, the Lord cancelled the promise he made to his posterity. Here is how God explained his change of plans for his family:[12]

> "Therefore the LORD, the God of Israel, declares: 'I promised that members of your family would minister before me forever.' But now the LORD declares: 'Far be it from me! Those who honor me I will honor, but those who despise me will be disdained.'"

 And we can add the testimony of Ellen White who issued a very serious warning a century ago to the Adventist community when she was informed that adultery and fornication were taking place among God's chosen people, and let's bear in mind that she said this at a time when Adventists were still pro-life:[13]

> "We must as a people arouse and cleanse the camp of Israel. Licentiousness, unlawful intimacy, and unholy practices are coming in among us in a large degree; and ministers who are handling sacred things are guilty of sin in this respect.
>
> They are coveting their neighbors' wives, and the seventh commandment is broken. We are in danger of becoming a sister to fallen Babylon, of allowing our churches to become corrupted, and filled with every foul spirit, a cage for every unclean and hateful bird; and will we be clear unless we make decided movements to cure the existing evil?"

---

[12] 1 Sam. 2:30
[13] 21MR 380.1

Is Our Situation Hopeless?

 Given our dire moral situation, you may ask: Is our Adventist situation hopeless? My answer is no! When King David realized that he was guilty of murder, he repented and leaned on God's mercy. He was guilty of one murder; we are guilty of the killing of thousands innocent victims of abortion, children who were entitled to life, but we gave them the opposite: death by dismemberment or poisoning, and we profited from those murders.

King David was called by God to a noble work, and he was credited with victories over incredible odds. He freed God's chosen people from suffering and oppression and laid the foundation for the glorious future experienced by the nation of Israel under his leadership and that of his son Solomon.

Then, at the height of his reign, he experienced a terrible moral fall; but he repented of this sin and God extended his pardon and mercy towards him. Likewise, the Adventist Church had a glorious beginning and God entrusted it with the last message of hope to a world engulfed in moral darkness.

The church managed to build hundreds of educational institutions around the world and a large number of medical facilities bringing hope and a healthier lifestyle to thousands around the world.

The Lord blessed the Adventist's efforts on behalf of suffering humanity. Unfortunately, when the big test came; the Adventist leaders yielded to the temptation of adding killing to our healing ministry. This must stop! We cannot continue violating God's moral Law with impunity

The Lord is patient and merciful, but if we do not repent of our great sin, he will spit us out of his mouth as described in the last book of the Bible. This book is written with the hope that we will exhibit, like King David, the right response. We need to say with David:[14]

---

[14] Psalm 32

13

> *1Blessed is the one whose transgressions are forgiven, whose sins are covered.*
>
> *2Blessed is the one whose sin the Lord does not count against them and in whose spirit is no deceit.*
>
> *3When I kept silent, my bones wasted away through my groaning all day long.*
>
> *4For day and night your hand was heavy on me; my strength was sapped as in the heat of summer.*
>
> *5Then I acknowledged my sin to you and did not cover up my iniquity. I said, "I will confess my transgressions to the Lord." And you forgave the guilt of my sin.*

This book was written with this goal in mind. May God's Holy Spirit lead his chosen people towards said objective! There is still time to admit our corporate moral guilt and with a contrite heart seek God's mercy and forgiveness for this great sin.

THE WAY WE ARE

A Vigorous Debate

 Many young Adventists are not aware that the way we are is not the way we were. When the Adventist leadership granted carte blanche to the denominationally owned and operated medical institutions to provide abortions on demand to their patients back in 1970, the result was a vigorous debate which lasted a couple of decades over the wisdom of this decision.

 A good example of the strong defense mounted by some of the Adventist pro-life leaders can be seen in an article written by George Gainer, who described in minutest details the history of how our church moved from a pro-life position to a pro-choice/pro-abortion one. His article was published by *"Ministry"* on August 1991 with the following title *"Abortion: history of Adventist guidelines."*[15]

Many Adventists, especially those who were born after 1973, the year the killing of the unborn was legalized in the U.S., believe that our Adventist attitude on the right to life has always been pro-choice instead of pro-life.

This could not be farther from the truth. There was a fundamental shift in our view of the sanctity of human life, and this drastic change took place in 1970—three years before the legalization of abortion in the U.S. mainland.

Recently, Martin Weber wrote the following comment dealing with this vigorous debate in Adventistm:[16]

---

[15] https://www.ministrymagazine.org/archive/1991/08/abortion-history-of-adventist-guidelines
[16] http://advindicate.com/articles/3236

> *"Nic, God bless you (and everybody else reading this) for your efforts regarding life. I've been fighting this battle for 30 years and it's been kind of lonely, except for faithful friends like George Gainer and David Newman. We at Ministry magazine fought so hard in 1992 at the GC Annual Council, both by putting out a special pro-life issue of Ministry (Sept. 92) and on the floor as delegates. Our efforts utterly failed, but at least we did our best for God."*

My personal investigation into this issue[17] revealed that two thirds of Adventists were opposed to the new liberal policy that allowed the killing of innocent unborn babies with impunity in our own hospitals.

Many voices among Adventism clamored for a strict pro-life response to this crisis, but the church opted to grant the power to draft guidelines on abortion to the Loma Linda University.

A Flawed Decision

 This decision was unwise, in my opinion. How could an entity that had a vested interest in the profit derived from abortion and transplantation adopt an objective view of the issues involved? Would anyone trust the tobacco industry to draft the policies connected with the production, distribution, promotion, and use of tobacco products?

The result was the adoption of our current document known as *"Guidelines on Abortion,"[18]* which is a hybrid declaration of both the sanctity of human life and women's right to abortion under a large variety of circumstances which include rape, incest, malformation, threat to the woman's life, and even the mental health of a pregnant woman.

---

[17]
http://www.lulu.com/shop/search.ep?type=&keyWords=nic+samojluk&sitesearch=lulu.com&q=&x=12&y=12
[18] http://www.adventist.org/information/official-statements/guidelines/article/go/0/abortion/6/

This means that the abortion option would be available to women all the way to the moment of birth. All a woman needed to do was to show evidence that her mental health was being affected by the pregnancy. This is evident from the Doe v Bolton legal case.[19]

Have you ever seen a woman mentally unaffected by an unwanted pregnancy, especially if she is unmarried, young, without financial means to support herself and her baby, or in the middle of her studies? Do you think that it would be difficult for such a woman to convince an abortionist to provide an abortion for her? All she needs to say is: *"This pregnancy drives me nuts; I can't concentrate on my studies, I can't sleep, and I am mentally depressed."*

A Deceptive Label

Can someone tell me how is this policy different from the one espoused by the rest of society? We describe this policy as *"pro-choice."* In fact there is very little difference between the pro-choice and the pro-abortion positions. They are the same enchilada with a slightly different label.

Many women who would prefer to carry their pregnancy to completion are prevented by their boy friends, relatives, and by their lack of funds from exercising this kind of choice. This means that many women have very little real choice in the matter. They are surrounded by circumstances that make them powerless to exercise real choice.

Besides, how about the choice of the unborn? True choice would require the consent of the main victim in these situations: the unborn. Is the interest of the unborn being considered? Of course not! The result is that the selfish interest of others prevails over the right to life of the unborn.

---

[19] "This health exception expanded the right to abortion for any reason through all three trimesters of pregnancy." http://www.mccl.org/Page.aspx?pid=323

17

A Mysterious Silence

Following the adoption of our current abortion guidelines in 1992, our Adventist media lost interest in continuing the debate about abortion. Many pro-life Adventist leaders left the church; some of them started their own independent ministries; and, believe it or not, some even went as far as joining the Catholic organization due to its strong pro-life position.

 Our official *"Ministry"* magazine, which had been following this controversial debate for many years, suddenly went into a long hibernation and refused to publish anything that dealt with the issue. I suggest the special report I wrote about this unusual event entitled *"The Day Ministry Magazine Went Silent on Abortion."* [20]

No Equal Time for Pro-lifers

Some Adventist media entities limited themselves to occasionally publishing articles and comments favoring the new so called *"pro-choice"* position. On more than one occasion, I requested equal time to speak in defense of the right to life of the unborn, and was told that the topic was controversial. Well, the topic seemed not to be controversial until I asked for a chance to present the opposite view.

I encountered a fierce opposition to my efforts to publish my views on this controversial topic. The Adventist apathy towards the plight of the unborn was so great, I feared I would never be heard unless I attach a Ph.D. title to my name. This led me back to school, which forced me to study part time online, and after a decade I was able to get my first article published by an Adventist journal.

Between 1971 and 1996 I counted 95 Readers' comments and articles dealing with abortion in the pages of our *"Ministry"* magazine. The readers' interest in this controversial issue was so great that on July 1988 David Newman wrote the following:[21]

---

[20] http://adventlife.wordpress.com/2012/02/05/hello-world/
[21] J. David Newman, "First Glance" *Ministry* (July 1988): 3.

> *"Our articles on abortion have touched a sensitive nerve. We are receiving more email on this subject than on any other recently published article. The letters are running 10 to 1 in favor of the church adopting a stricter standard."*

Then suddenly, a few years following the publication of our current Adventist *"Guidelines on Abortion"* a long silence ensued on the pages of this periodical.

A News Blackout

 What happened? Why the sudden silence? Did the interest in abortion diminish, or was this the result of an intentional desire by the pro-choice elite and the liberal leadership to silence the pro-life opposition whose opinions were running, according to Newman, *"10 to 1 in favor of the church adopting a stricter standard"* I cannot be 100 percent sure, but the timing of the comments on abortion blackout is rather suspicious!

I did perform an exhaustive investigation about this topic and discovered that two thirds of our Adventists who were active in expressing their opinions in our publications were on the pro-life side of the issue, while one third of the Adventist leaders and article writers were favoring a pro-choice agenda. The church granted the power to draft our guidelines on abortion to the latter group, and they prevailed in this moral controversy.

My guess is that the members of the Adventist intelligentsia must have realized that if the freedom of the press was allowed to continue, their favored views on abortion might eventually be in danger of collapsing under the weight of those advanced by pro-lifers through the pages of our Adventist periodicals.

THE WAY WE WERE

Our pioneers Attitude Towards Abortion

I would like to start this chapter with a brief description of the SDA pioneer's attitude towards Abortion. This will take us back to 1870, slightly over a century before the U.S. Supreme Court removed the protection from the unborn, thus legalizing the practice of abortion.

What was the Seventh-day Adventist forefathers' attitude towards the destruction of human life prior to natural birth? At that time, one of the most prolific spokesmen for the nascent Adventist movement was James White, the founder of the SDA publishing work and also president of the General Conference of Seventh-day Adventists.

Here is what he included in a book he published; and it is important to remember that at no time his wife, Ellen G. White, the widely accepted messenger of the Lord for the new religious movement, attempted to negate or soften up the message contained in the following crystal clear pro-life declaration:[22]

The Opinion Published by James White.

> *"Few are aware of the fearful extent to which this nefarious business, this worse than devilish practice, is carried on in all classes of society! Many a woman determines that she will not become a mother, and subjects herself to the vilest treatment, committing the basest crime to carry out her purpose. And many a man, who has as many children as he can support, instead of restraining his passions, aids in the destruction of the babes he has begotten.*

---

[22] James White. *Solemn Appeal* (Battle Creek, Michigan: Stem Press, 1870), 100.

> *The sin lies at the door of both parents in equal measure; for the father, although he may not always aid in the murder, is always accessory to it, in that he induces, and sometimes even forces upon the mother the condition which he knows will lead to the commission of the crime."*

Do these statements published by James White, the founder of the SDA printing work and president of the SDA church, sound like pro-life statements? They evidently do! Are there any references in them to a woman's right to choose between life and death for the developing baby? Not a chance! Do they contain any indication that there might exist some exceptions in the event the pregnant woman is not mature enough to raise the child after delivery, or if the parents already have enough mouths to care for and feed? Certainly not!

Are there any euphemisms in James declaration such as *"pregnancy interruption," "product of conception,"* or *"reproductive freedom?"* The answer is No. James White did not feel there was a need to soften the terms he used for abortion, and labeled this practice as *"murder."* This is important to notice, because the purpose of this study is to discover the true attitude of Adventists towards the practice of abortion when the church was young and growing in order to determine whether the SDA Church still holds these values in high esteem; or whether perhaps there has been since then a significant departure from the pro-life attitude towards abortion manifested by the early SDA pioneers.

Were there any other voices among Adventists speaking on the subject? The answer is yes. Actually, *"Between 1850 and 1890 in this country, the medical community led a campaign to outlaw abortion except to save the life of the mother,"*[23] and notable SDA torchbearers heartily supported such a campaign. Here are some statements by leading members of the nascent SDA church as evidence that this religious community was not silent on the issue of abortion:

---

[23] P.A. Lorenz. *Adventist For Life News,* Vol. III, Issue 3 (n.d., Heritage Edition): 3.

Statements by John Harvey Kellogg[24]

"The idea held by many that the destruction of foetal [sic] life is not a crime until after "quickening" has occurred is a gross and mischievous error. No change occurs in the developing human being at this period.

The so-called period of "quickening" is simply the period at which the movements of the little one become sufficiently active and vigorous to attract the attention of the mother. Long before this, slight movements have been taking place, and from the very moment of conception, those processes have been in operation which result in the production of a fully developed human being from a mere jelly drop, a minute cell.

As soon as this development begins, a new human being has come into existence–in embryo, it is true, but possessed of its own individuality, with its own future, its possibilities of joy, grief, success, failure, fame, and ignominy."

Who wrote the above quoted statements? Those declarations were made by the most influential SDA physician at that time, the one groomed by Ellen G. White to be the founder of the Adventist medical work. There is no need to emphasize the fact that he was definitely and unambiguously on the pro-life side of this issue. His choice of words, and the emphasis he placed on them, suggests that his opposition to the practice of abortion was even stronger than those in the pro-life movement today.

He minced no adjectives in expressing his profound aversion to the destruction of human life from the moment of conception.[25] But there is

---

[24] J.H. Kellogg. *Man the Masterpiece* (Battle Creek, Michigan: Modern Medicine Publishing Co., 1894), 424-425. Also John Harvey Kellogg. "Infanticide and Abortion" *Plain Facts for Old and/Electronic Text Center/Young/University of Virginia Library.*
http://etext.lib.virginia.edu/etcbin/toccer-
new2?id=KelPlai.sgm&images=images/modeng&data=/texts/english/modeng/parsed&tag=pu
blic&part=21&division=div1

more. Let us consider what J. N. Andrews, the first Seventh-day Adventist missionary ever sent abroad had to say on the subject; followed by the opinions of John Todd and Uriah Smith, who for many decades was the editor of the *Advent Review and Sabbath Herald,* the forerunner of our current official magazine—*The Adventist Review.*

As you read what these Adventist pioneers wrote about the respect for human life, you probably wonder how we Adventists could have taken such a drastic detour from the right path. We have made a similar mistake to that of the Jewish nation: They emphasized the sacredness of one of God's Commandments while ignoring the mandate of another one. The Sabbath is sacred no doubt, but human life is sacred as well. In fact Jesus told us that the Sabbath was made for man, and not the reverse. The Jews killed an innocent man and rushed home to keep the Sabbath Holy.

The Thinking of J.N. Andrews, John Todd, & Uriah Smith[26]

> *"One of the most shocking, and yet one of the most prevalent sins of this generation, is the murder of unborn infants. Let those who think this a small sin, read Ps. 139:16. They will see that even the unborn child is written in God's book. And they may be well assured that God will not pass unnoticed the murder of such children."*

These strong words came from the pen of J. N. Andrews, editor of the original official magazine published by the SDA church. There is no doubt that he was a strong supporter of the sanctity of human life from the moment of conception. Andrews' views on abortion were supported by another influential writer of the fast growing pro-life religious movement: John Todd.[27]

---

[25] For additional details about Dr. Kelloggs' unswerving opposition of abortion, see Dalton Baldwin's article discussed in Chapter VIII of my first book on abortion.

[26] J.N. Andrews, ed. "A Few Words Concerning a Great Sin" *Advent Review and Sabbath Herald* (30 Nov. 1869): 184.

[27] John Todd. "Fashionable Murder" *Advent Review and Sabbath Herald* (25 June 1867): 29.

"Nothing but an imperative sense of duty could induce me to pen what I am about to write. Letters from different sections of the country, and from physicians too, are so urgent that I should write on this subject, that I may not choose. I have no fear but what I am about to write will be read; but I wish it might be solemnly pondered. I am about to speak, and plainly too, of the practice of producing abortions.

As a class, the medical profession have taken a noble stand. The desolations have become so fearful that, as the guardians of human life, they are compelled to do so: and society owes a debt of gratitude to Dr. H.R. Storer, of Boston, especially for his powerful arguments, lucid arrangements of facts, patient investigations and earnest and eloquent remonstrances.

Among his writings on this subject, the little work entitled "Why Not?" Is a "book for every woman," and I do wish that women might carefully read it. If any of my lady readers shall complain of a want of delicacy, I beg them to remember three facts; first, that the practice is fearfully common; second, that probably they are every week associating with those who are guilty of the practice; and third, that seventy-five per cent of all the abortions produced are caused and effected by females. What then of delicacy?

As to guilt, I want all to know that, in the sight of God, it is willful murder. "The willful killing of a human being at any stage of its existence, is murder.

It might be proper to add a statement by Uriah Smith, the renowned SDA scholar and writer who edited the *Advent Review and Sabbath Herald* for 40 years. Although he does not refer specifically to the issue of abortion, yet his reference to the SDA publishing norms at the time gives us a glimpse about what the early pioneers thought regarding involvement in politically controversial issues. Considering the emphatic condemnation of the practice of abortion by the above-mentioned SDA pioneers, the following statement by Uriah Smith becomes relevant to the topic under investigation.[28]

> *"You show me a church that fails to take a stand on political issues that involve moral principles, and I'll show you a church that is spineless, irrelevant, and morally bankrupt. ...No issue is too controversial for us to address and honestly in pages of our church paper."*

Statements by Ellen G. White

It is true that Ellen G. White in her prolific writing career spanning seven decades never addressed the issue of abortion in a clear and specific manner. Nevertheless, it is important to consider the following undeniable facts that reveal her attitude towards the moral value of human life prior to the moment of birth:

A. She never attempted to either contradict or soften the strong opinion of her husband on the subject, who occupied the position of General Conference President of the SDA Church.

---

[28] Uriah Smith. *Advent Review and Sabbath Herald.* Quoted by P.A. Lorenz. *Adventist for Life News,* Vol. III, Issue 3. (n.d., Heritage Edition): 3.

B. She worked with James White, her husband, in the SDA publishing work as hand and glove right from the beginning.

C. Several statements of her provide us a clue as to what her position regarding the sacredness of human life was and what her attitude towards the practice of abortion might have been:[29]

> *"Life is mysterious and sacred. It is the manifestation of God Himself, the source of all life. Precious are its opportunities, and earnestly should they be improved. Once lost, they are gone forever."*
>
> *"Human life, which God alone could give, must be sacredly guarded."*
>
> *"Children derive life from their parents, and yet it is through the creative power of God that your children have life, for God is the Life-giver."*

It is important to notice as well her many statements dealing with the relevance of prenatal care and the influence of the pregnant woman's diet, general health, mental attitude, and self control on the development of the unborn.[30]

> *"The effect of prenatal influence is by many parents looked upon as a matter of little moment; but heaven does not so regard it."*

But the most revealing comment found in the writings of Ellen White regarding her attitude toward abortion is probably the following:

---

[29] Ellen G. White. *Ministry of Healing* (Mountain View, California: Pacific Press Publishing Association, 1958), 397; White. *Patriarchs and Prophets* (Mountain View, California: Pacific Press Publishing Association, 1958), 516; White. *The Adventist Home* (Nashville, Tennessee: Southern Publishing Association, 1952), 280.

[30] Ibid., 257; White. *Ministry of Healing,* 373; Ibid., 372-373; White. *Selected Messages,* Vol. 2 (Washington, D.C.: Review and Herald Publishing Association, 1958), 429-430.

> *"If the father would become acquainted with physical law, he might better understand his obligations and responsibilities. He would see that he had been guilty of almost murdering his children, by suffering so many burdens to come upon the mother, compelling her to labor beyond her strength before their birth, in order to obtain means to leave for them."*

If Ellen White, the most influential leader of the SDA Church, was so concerned about the influence of the expectant mother upon the unborn and the harm the developing baby might suffer during the nine months of pregnancy, logical thinking might reasonably lead us to conclude that dismembering the little creature's body or poisoning it to death would be condemned by her even in stronger terms. Notice that she equates forcing a pregnant woman to work beyond her strength and endurance with ***"almost murdering his children."***

Then the question arises: What adjective would she have used for the actual killing of the unborn? Would it not be murder? Is there room here to avoid this logical conclusion? What force then remains in the argument claiming that Ellen G. White was silent on abortion? Perhaps the reader might ask the following question: Why was she silent on the abortion issue? Is there an explanation for her silence? What were the societal, political, and religious circumstances that might have prompted her to abstain from talking about the subject? Here is what P.A. Lorenz had to say in answer to these questions:[31]

> *"Perhaps one reason why she was silent on the practice of abortion in her day was because there was no need for her to say anything--the medical profession led a very vocal and successful campaign to prohibit abortion."*

Would Ellen White have remained silent on the issue of abortion had she disagreed with the then prevalent thinking about the subject?

---

[31] P.A. Lorenz, 3.

> *"The religious community, as a whole, also agreed that abortion should be prohibited. The Adventist Church leadership also spoke against abortion, as did the majority of society. It was simply not the controversy it is today, nor was it as widespread as it is today.*
>
> *Her silence must be interpreted in light of the circumstances of her time-- there is no evidence that there was any disagreement in the early Adventist Church on this issue."*

Would she have spoken on the subject had she deviated from her husband's strong opinion on abortion? She probably would! Therefore, what we need to consider is not her silence, but rather what she would have said today, given our drastically changed circumstances regarding this hotly contested topic. But notice what Ellen White stated about shortening human life, as well as indulging in passions that might lead to injurious acts towards others:[32]

Doesn't abortion shorten human life by an entire life span? How about the uncontrolled sexual activity with total disregard to the fact that such action will likely lead to harming the baby in case of pregnancy?

Tentative Conclusion

The above considerations seem to indicate that at the time of the pioneers, the Seventh-day Adventist community was neither pro-abortion, nor pro-choice, but rather pro-life. There is a striking absence of any pro-abortion or pro-choice arguments in the SDA literature of said period, coupled with a clear and unambiguous condemnation of abortion, and supported by convincing arguments dealing with the sanctity of human life before birth from the pen of Ellen G. White, the most prolific pioneer spokesperson of the Seventh-day Adventist Church.

---

[32] White. *Patriarchs and Prophets* (Washington, D.C.: Review and Herald Publishing Association, 1958), 316.

THINGS I LEARNED I N GRADUATE SCHOOL

Ten Lessons I Learned in Graduate School

 I have in my personal library a well known book authored by Robert Fulghum entitled *All I Really Need to Know I Learned in Kindergarten.* I could not make such a claim because my parents did not enroll me in it. This is why I have opted to rather talk about what I learned in graduate school about abortion and the Seventh-day Adventist Church. These things I learned as the result of the topic I chose for my doctoral dissertation entitled: *From Pro-life to Pro-choice: The Dramatic Shift in Seventh-day Adventists' Attitudes Towards Abortion.*[33]

- **Lesson One:** Both our nation and the Adventist Church were founded on the solid foundation of respect for God, the Creator, and a high regard for his Law. Even today Moses and the Ten Commandments are enshrined in the Halls of the U.S. Supreme Court.
- **Lesson Two:** Both our nation and the Adventist Church have recently demonstrated a lack of respect towards such emblems of our loyalty to our Creator. This has recently become very apparent in our diminished respect for the moral value of human life.
- **Lesson Three:** When both our nation and the Adventist Church were founded, the practice of abortion was considered to be equivalent to murder. Today, if someone kills a wanted unborn baby, it is treated as murder; but if the baby is unwanted, no crime has been committed and we call such a violent act *"therapy."* Of course, nobody is lining up in order to receive such therapy for himself.
- **Lesson Four:** If a woman is raped, we let the guilty live, but kill the innocent baby and call this an example of our fairness and

33

http://www.lulu.com/shop/search.ep?type=&keyWords=nic+samojluk&sitesearch=lulu.com&
q=&x=12&y=12

compassion. Since when is killing the innocent an act of compassion? Of course, no one is eager to be the recipient of this kind of compassion.

- **Lesson Five:** Our ancestors killed in time of war; we kill both in times of war and in peace time.
- **Lesson Six:** Our ancestors killed in order to preserve their own lives; we kill to preserve our lifestyle.
- **Lesson Seven:** They killed out of a sense of duty; we kill in order to avoid our moral duty.
- **Lesson Eight:** They killed their enemies; we kill our own children at a time when they are most vulnerable.
- **Lesson Nine:** According to experts, six decades ago, our nation was the largest creditor in the entire world. Today the U.S. is the largest debtor, and our greatest creditor is an officially Communist country. I thought we had defeated Communism! My state—California—is financially broke, the city of Detroit has filed for bankruptcy, and the federal government is likewise on the edge of bankruptcy.
- **Lesson Ten:** Our Adventist pioneers had a high respect for all Ten of God's Commandments. Today our church has watered down beyond recognition the true and original meaning of the Sixth Commandments that forbids the killing of innocent human beings. Some of our own medical institutions have been killing unwanted babies by the hundreds and even perform elective abortions on babies perfectly formed.

Other Lessons I Learned in Graduate School

 I also learned that the abortion crisis in our Adventist church is mainly a North American phenomenon. An old friend of mine did inform me that abortion was not permitted in the Adventist medical institutions under his care when he was in charge of our medical work in Europe, Africa, and South America. No wonder our church is not growing in the U.S., but has been growing by leaps and bounds in some of those countries. How can a church that kills its own children prosper and grow?

30

 I discovered that we get a knee jerk reaction every time Sunday laws are in the news, which so far is killing nobody, but have a blind spot to real killers like abortion. We go to the ends of the earth to convince people that the true Sabbath is sacred, but forget that Human life is also sacred. Didn't Jesus say that the Sabbath was made for man, and not the reverse, thus implying that human life is holy likewise?

We have invested tons of time and ink in order to help those addicted to tobacco product quit the habit, because such a change in lifestyle tends to add five years to their life, but have no interest in the pro-life movement which adds between 80 and 90 years of life to the abortion victims.

When a baby is born with a defective heart, we have no regret making over a six figure dollar investment to save the baby's life, but turn a blind eye when other Adventist physicians are killing well formed and healthy babies by the hundreds—many of them in our own medical facilities.

 Hitler killed six million Jews, and we call this genocide; Americans killed nearly sixty million innocent unborn human beings and we call it an expression of our freedom of choice. We teach that Jesus died to free us from sin, and we also teach that he died to grant us the freedom to choose—to kill innocent babies under a variety of circumstances, including when the woman is faced with an unplanned pregnancy, gets depressed and her *"mental health"* is affected.

We have lofty pro-life statements in our official document entitled *Guidelines on Abortion*,[34] but we loaded the document with many exceptions that make the pro-life pronouncements null and void for all practical purposes. Would it make any sense to state that stealing a car is wrong; except when the burglar is unemployed, when his own car has broken down, when it is an emergency, or when his neighbor has more vehicles than he needs?

---

[34] http://www.adventist.org/beliefs/guidelines/main-guide1.html

 We have redefined the true meaning of death. When an anencephalic baby is born, we say the baby is brain dead in spite of the fact that the baby is alive and is breathing and kicking. Why do we do this? Because this allows us to remove the baby's vital organs before the baby is really dead in order to facilitate our transplantation program. Wouldn't it make more sense to save the lives of those healthy babies who are being poisoned or dismembered by the thousands every week by abortionists?

Can you guess why we switched from a strong pro-life position to a pro-choice/pro-abortion one? Profit, fear of loosing patients and staff, fear of financial insolvency; in essence, fear of men, but a lack of fear of God. I learned this by reading the Adventist history as recorded in our own publications. I also learned that two thirds of our magazine readers were on the pro-life side of his controversial issue, but the power was in the hands of the liberal minded leaders of the church.

These things I learned, and much more, when I decided to sign up for a doctoral program in religion. Why did I do this given my advanced age and my very limited financial resources? Because the church closed all avenues for me when I tried to speak on behalf of the unborn. Our Adventist pro-choice leaders were allowed to ridicule pro-lifers and, every time I requested equal time to speak in defense of the most vulnerable members of humanity, I was informed that the topic was controversial. It was not controversial when they spoke in defense of abortion, but it became controversial the moment I opened my mouth!

 I wrote letters to the former General Conference president and the current one, and I am still waiting for a response. Every time I sent a financial contribution to our Adventist pro-life cause, my checks were returned with the following message: *"The Adventist Church does not have a pro-life program."* In my desperation, I decided that if I secure a Ph.D. degree, perhaps I might be able to get a word edgewise on behalf of those who cannot speak for themselves.

 Some years ago, a former president of Andrews University was teaching a Loma Linda University Church Sabbath School and he presented some controversial doctrines to us. A former student of his asked: *"How come you never said anything about this when you were our president"*? *"I didn't want to rock the boat!"* he responded. Every time I speak on behalf of the unborn, some Adventists advise me not to rock the boat. If our boat is about to hit an iceberg, is it wrong to rock the boat? Should the captain say, I am not going to rock the boat; some of the passengers may feel dizzy?

A few years ago, a pro-life friend of mine asked his pastor why he never preached about sin and abortion. *"If I did that, some of my members might get offended,"* he replied. Can you imagine John the Baptist, the Old Testament prophets, or Jesus saying this as an excuse for not preaching against sin? The Bible compares such preachers to dogs who won't ark. As I was handing a pro-life piece of literature to a Sabbath School member, a dear Adventist sister shouted with anger: *"You are doing the Devil's work."* Perhaps those prophets who called sin by its right name were also doing the Devil's work!

 Should we sanitize the Bible and delete from the sacred pages the story of David's sin, Peter's denial of Jesus, and books like Judges? I wish some of the things I found in the holy pages of our official *Ministry* magazine were not there; but they are part of our history. This is the source I gleaned a great portion of the material I used for my doctoral dissertation. I do know that we can catch more flies with honey than with vinegar; nevertheless someone has to shake the beehive to collect the honey and risk getting a few stings in the process. As you read this, I would like you to do so with the following probing question in you mind:

Should the Adventist Church get out of the abortion business and disconnect itself from any Adventist medical institution that is unwilling to do likewise and thus let such entities go their own way to become totally autonomous and start operating as independent ministries similar to *"The Quiet Hour"* and *"3ABN"*?

My prayer and my hope is towards that end! May the good Lord bless you as you read this book which was prepared with a great deal of sadness, dedication, hope and personal sacrifice.

More:====> If this topic is of interest to you, I suggest you secure a copy of the first book I published on this topic entitled: *"From Pro-life to Pro-choice: The Dramatic Shift in Seventh-day Adventists' Attitudes Towards Abortion."* [35]

The Broken Blueprint

Someone may ask: How could a pro-life denomination depart so far from the right path and embrace the murder of the unborn for filthy profit? The answer may be found in a book entitled ***"The Broken Blueprint"*** authored by Vance Ferrell. Right from the start, Ellen White advised the leaders of the Adventist church not to associate with unbelievers in their medical work. This biblical principle was ignored by those in power, and the managers of our medical institutions did secure the services of non-Adventist physicians in an attempt at competing with the rest of the world.

The first move was to offer the so-called therapeutic abortion. By the time the State of Hawaii decided to legalize elective abortions, our Castle Memorial Hospital [CMH] was already offering said kind of abortion. The hospital had been constructed with large donations from the public, and the hospital administrators promised that they would offer full medical services to the community.

 Shortly after the legalization of abortion in said state, a man who had donated $25,000 dollars for the construction of CMH requested an abortion for his daughter. Half of the physicians employed by the hospital--who were not members of the Adventist Church--requested the right to offer abortions on demand to their patients. When management refused, they threatened to take their patients elsewhere. The request was elevated to the

[35]

http://www.lulu.com/shop/search.ep?type=&keyWords=nic+samojluk&sitesearch=lulu.com&
q=&x=12&y=12

Pacific Union first and eventually to the North American Division [NAD] of the church.

The leadership of the church panicked, the fear of the Lord was replaced with the fear of men and the fear of loss of revenue, and the church decided to cave in to the demands and thus compromise with evil. This decision was mirrored in a public statement made by Neal Wilson, the then president of the NAD:[36]

> *"Though we walk the fence, SDAs lean towards abortion rather than against it. Because we realize we are confronted with big problems of hunger and over-population, we do not oppose family planning and appropriate endeavors to control population.*

Can you imagine the import of such a statement by the leader of the church in North America? An admission that it is morally justified to start killing the most innocent members of the human race because there was too much hunger in the world and too many people? And let's not forget that Wilson was saying this in the richest nation of the world where the lack of food was not a problem! Eventually, other Adventist hospitals decided to mimic what CMH was doing, and at least five other hospitals began offering elective abortion services to their communities.[37]

What I Learned About Abortion & the SDA Church

The following is a summary of the most important discoveries I made after carefully reviewing the Adventist literature dealing with this topic. Some of these things may surprise you, but they reflect what Adventists have published in our own books and periodicals. One of the major sources of information came from magazines such as *"Ministry"* and *"Spectrum."* By

---

[36] George Gainer, The Wisdom of Solomon? *Spectrum* 19/4 (May 1989): 38-46.
[37] Gerald R. Winslow, "Abortion Policies in Adventist Hospitals" Specttum 19/4 (May 1989): 47-50.

the way, the material published by Spectrum was less liberal a few decades ago than what it is today.

Here is a summary of what I learned from my research. From the moment of its inception the members of the Seventh-day Adventist [SDA] religious denomination portrayed themselves as the apocalyptic Remnant that keeps the commandments of God in the midst of almost universal apostasy.

 One of those commandments clearly forbids killing, yet abortions are taking place inside SDA medical institutions, both therapeutic and even elective in some of them, while conflicting statements are made by leading officials of the church, with the former president of the General Conference of the Seventh-day Adventist affirming that the SDA church is pro-life. To elucidate this apparently enigmatic contradiction, I decided to investigate this incongruous ethical situation, and made the following discoveries:

- The early SDA pioneers manifested a most determined opposition to abortion.
- Two thirds of those who did express their opinions in the leading, recently published, SDA books and periodicals seemed to be on the pro-life side of this issue, but lacked the power to set the official policy of the church.
- The leaders of the church delegated the decision power dealing with abortion to the ethicists connected with the medical institutions of the church.
- Most SDA owned hospitals were providing therapeutic abortion several years before the legalization of abortion.
- Fear of revenue loss prompted some SDA hospitals to offer abortion on demand in response to the demands of non-Adventists physicians employed by the church.
- One of these church-owned institutions was recently labeled as an *"abortion mill"* by a leading church official.
- When pressed for an official statement by the church back in 1970, Neal Wilson, the president of the North American Division of Seventh-day Adventists at the time predicted that the church would adopt a pro-choice position regarding abortion,

and rationalized said practice as a reasonable way to control the world hunger and population.

- The official *Guidelines on Abortion* document voted by the church seems to be a mixture of lofty pro-life statements mingled with pro-choice exceptions that render the apparently pro-life policy meaningless.
- Said official *Guidelines on Abortion* are non-prescriptive in nature, and each SDA institution is free to set their own policies dealing with abortion.
- Official church documents call for the protection of human life, but a leading SDA ethicist has declared that the church has decided not to pinpoint when human life begins.
- Several of the leading pro-life movers within the SDA church have since left the community in order to pursue their independent ministries.
- There has been a seemingly dramatic shift in the SDA church's attitude towards the sanctity of human life immediately prior and following the legalization of abortion by the Supreme Court of the United States of America.

A PRO-LIFE ADVENTIST HERO

 Before we continue the discussion of this extremely relevant topic, it might be helpful to paint a picture of SDA's attitude towards the sanctity of human life a few decades before the U.S. Supreme Court removed the legal protection from the unborn and legalized the practice of abortion. I would like to accomplish this by telling a story. It is the story of a SDA soldier who was drafted for military service during World War II.

His name was Desmond T. Doss, a young man who had registered as a Conscientious Objector (I-A-O). Why did he register under the I-A-O designation?

Because he was a practicing SDA, and one of his strongest religious convictions was the respect for the sacredness of human life, together with a high respect for the sacredness of God's Holy Day–the Seventh Day of the week, or Sabbath; and a deep deference towards the other precepts of the Decalogue.

The story of this soldier illustrates the attitude of SDA's towards the sacredness of human life at that time. In those days, men who served in the army as conscientious objectors were held in rather low esteem, were often ridiculed by their comrades, and mistreated by their superiors. Some of them were abused, imprisoned, assigned to menial tasks, kicked and beaten, and even *"dunked headfirst into latrines."*

During the war, 162 members of the Seventh-day Adventist Church were court-martialed because of their religious convictions, and when the war ended, thirty-five of these men were serving terms of from five to twenty years at hard labor."[38]

---

[38] Booton Herndon. *The Unlikeliest Hero* (Mountain View, California: Pacific Press Publishing Association, 1967), 16.

38

Desmond Doss Military Training

Desmond Doss was well aware of this unfortunate situation, but his religious convictions were ingrained in his soul since childhood, and he could not bear the thought of taking the life of another human being–not even in self defense during wartime. He wanted to serve his country, but he determined he would refuse to bear arms as evidence of his respect for the sacredness of human life. He was drafted along with many other Adventist young men, and was assigned, by mistake, to a rifle company.

His first day in the army did not go well. When it was bedtime, he knelt beside his bunk bed in order to say his prayers, and all of a sudden he became the object of ridicule. A heavy army shoe sailed above his head. He didn't want to get hit by a shoe, but he didn't want to cut short his prayers. He realized he would need the Lord like never before.

In vain did the supply sergeant, the platoon sergeant, the platoon lieutenant, and the company captain attempted to make him carry a gun. No amount of begging, coaxing, or threatening was effective in altering his determination not to bear arms. He clearly remembered that[39]

> *"On the wall of the living room, back in the little frame house in Lynchburg, Virginia, [his hometown] hung a framed scroll depicting the Ten Commandments. ... Each commandment was illustrated by a drawing. The one that gripped him most concerned the sixth commandment: Thou shalt not kill. It depicted the story of Cain and Abel. In the illustration Abel lay on the ground bleeding, while over him stood the murderous Cain, dagger in hand."*

---

[39] Ibid., 12.

This illustration was fresh in his mind as he faced his superiors demanding that he obey their orders. When everything failed, Doss was reassigned to a group of soldiers being trained as medics. Sometimes the infantry engaged in rifle marksmanship training, and while the rest of the soldiers practiced, Doss stood around doing nothing. This was a cause for resentment among his fellow soldiers.

But this was not all. This SDA soldier also refused to do any work on his Holy Day, the seventh day of the week, or Sabbath. Of course, he was willing to perform his medical duties on his day of rest, but he refused to perform any ordinary assignment that could be done on any other day of the week like scrubbing the barracks floor for Saturday inspection. *"A floor can be scrubbed any day of the week,"* [40] he would argue.

 To compensate for his refusal to do menial work on the Sabbath, he willingly would work all day on Sundays, but none of the other young men were around to see him do this, and they resented the special treatment he was granted every Saturday. On his company's first training long march, Doss performed better than some of the other soldiers.

During the long trek, and that evening, he had the chance to treat the blistered feet of some of his comrades who had previously ridiculed and taunted him with profanity. That evening no profanity was heard in the barracks. Soon Doss befriended a Catholic named Glenn, who agreed to work for him on Saturdays so he could go to church on condition that he substitute for him on Sundays to allow him to attend Catholic mass.

Major Steinman, who was in charge of the medical battalion, became extremely angry at Doss' Sabbath privileges, and threatened to have him court-martialed; but no amount of coaxing or threats succeeded in breaking his determination to follow his conscience on this matter. Sometime later, one of his superiors notified him that he had discovered a way to get him out of the army by using mental instability as the reason for the discharge.

Doss could have grasped this opportunity to put an end to his trials; but he would not pretend to be insane, when in fact there was nothing wrong with

---

[40] Ibid., 24.

his mental state. He then was transferred to the infantry division, and one of his fellow soldiers told him he had betted ten dollars that the commander would not succeed in forcing Doss to carry a weapon. He won the bet and Captain Stanley lost.

Lieutenant Cosner tried hard to convince Doss that he must agree to carry a weapon, but failed. Finally he asked him: *"Suppose somebody was raping your wife. Wouldn't you use a gun?"* *"I wouldn't have one,"* he replied. *"What would you do, then?"* he asked. *"I wouldn't just stand there,"* he answered; *"I wouldn't use a gun, and wouldn't kill, but he'd sure wish he was dead when I got through with him."* At that time, he received a copy of a document signed by President Roosevelt stating that conscientious objectors did not have to bear arms. Doss was transferred back to the medic department of the army.

The 77th Infantry Division Guam Mission

 When his training was over, the time came for him to leave with his 77th Infantry Division sailing for Guam, which the Japanese had occupied shortly after their attack against Pearl Harbor. Colonel Gerald G. Cooney, knowing that Japanese soldiers were under directives to seek and kill medics, ordered Doss to carry a weapon; which order he refused, and almost got sent back to the states; but Captain Vernon intervened on Doss behalf and he was allowed to remain in the army. They had to disembark by jumping into the water, and managed to survive for four days in their cold, wet clothes. Then it started to rain, which means their clothes did not have a chance to dry up.

His first chance at using his medical training came when one of the soldiers picked an attractive fountain pen, which had been booby-trapped with explosives by the Japanese. In spite of the rain, the American soldiers did not have drinking water, which forced them to carry out an assault on a Japanese stronghold. Eighty-five men were either killed or wounded, which kept Doss pretty busy. He even provided first aid to one of the natives, and was reprimanded by his superiors.

He would quite often get separated from his platoon while tending to the injured, and would hurry to catch up with them while the enemy bullets and grenades made such an attempt extremely dangerous, but Doss felt he could not leave them without medical help. On one occasion, while the enemy fire was the heaviest, Doss demanded help from the sergeant to carry a wounded soldier. His superior thought this was suicidal, but Doss prevailed, and with the help of other soldiers the life of the badly wounded man was saved.

The Island of Leyte Wartime Mission

His army division's next military assignment was Leyte, where Doss experienced one of his most painful losses: He was called to tend to the wounds of Glenn, his Catholic friend who had substituted for him in order that he might attend Sabbath services at the local SDA church while in training. He rushed to his friend' side under heavy enemy fire; he felt for his pulse, but could detect none. His best friend, Clarence Glen, was dead and would not have a chance to say his last goodbye to his wife and baby. After that painful experience, Doss would never look at the face of a soldier while taking care of his wounds, fearing he might see again the face of another close friend.

 Doss was not getting enough nourishment and felt the pangs of hunger. Upon discovering some coconut trees, he climbed one of them–though exhausted–and threw down some of the coconuts. By the time he got down, the other soldiers had picked the last coconut and were gone. On another occasion, he moved toward another coconut tree behind a hedge, but gunfire erupted. It was an ambush. He ran and dove into a ditch, headfirst. He discovered empty bottles around. Evidently the Japanese soldier had been drinking and could not aim straight. Alcohol consumption by others had saved his life.

One day a call for help came from a wounded soldier. No one volunteered to go except Doss. *"Be careful,"* he was warned, *"The sniper that got him is still out there."*[41] Doss took care of the wounded man and helped him back to safety. A sergeant who watched the daring rescue stated:[42] *"Doss, I expected*

---

[41] Ibid., 81.
[42] Ibid., 82.

to see you killed any minute. We could all see it from up on the hill. You were crawling right toward that sniper."

Adventists later learned from the Japanese soldier that he was the sniper, and that he was determined to shoot as Doss crawled towards him. He attempted to pull the trigger, but couldn't. On one occasion Doss attempted to take care of a wounded Japanese soldier. One of the American soldiers told him that if he did that he would have to kill him. That was the only time he tried something like that.

As the Leyte military campaign grew to a close, one of those soldiers who had ridiculed Doss for his religious beliefs approached him. Doss expected some more of the same, but the distraught man blurted, *"Doss, pray for me."* *"I am no chaplain,"* responded Doss. The man answered that he had already talked to the army chaplain, but all he could offer him was a drink. Doss did pray for him, but that was the last time he saw him. At the conclusion of the Island of Leyte wartime mission, Doss was nominated for the Bronze Star.

The 77th Infantry Division's Okinawa Assignment

 When Doss' 77th Infantry Division approached the Island of Okinawa, the American soldiers learned that the Japanese had warned the native population that Americans would torture and slaughter them. To their horror, Doss and his comrades witnessed native women cutting their children's throats and then their own as the American forces approached.

Before their first assault of a Japanese position, Doss was told that there was no need for him to go, since it would be an extremely dangerous mission. He refused to stay behind. If the mission was risky, he was sure his comrades would need his medical services. Nevertheless, he suggested that they ask for God's guidance before attempting to scale the steep cliff.

He meant that everybody would offer a silent prayer, but his commanding officer asked Doss to publicly pray for the soldiers' safety. This operation was carried out with remarkable success, and with no serious wounds in spite of the hail of enemy bullets and grenades. Nevertheless, what followed kept Doss quite busy. One American soldier had barely reached out of his hole for his canteen when a bullet shot through his head.

Doss dragged the wounded soldier under heavy fire unscathed, but the wounded soldier died. Some of the American soldiers were decapitated by their enemies while sleeping in their holes. On one occasion Doss and his comrade found refuge in a cavern and agreed to take turns keeping watch. As Doss was keeping watch, he heard some whispering in Japanese from inside the hole. He could have used one of his comrades' grenades to put an end to the danger they were in, but he would not engage in killing.

Life in enemy's territory was extremely dangerous. Dorris, his medic partner, was wounded; and Doss suffered a fall over a parapet, injuring one of his legs. This predicament did not stop him from rendering his services to those who were in dire need of medical help. When Sabbath came, as he was reading his Bible, Captain Vernon informed him that he had orders to move across the hill to secure an enemy's position.

 "This is your Sabbath, you don't have to go," said the captain. *"I will go,"* responded Doss, *"if you let me finish my Bible reading."*[43] The captain with his company agreed to wait for him. At that moment, *"the entire American advance in Okinawa, a line several miles across and involving several divisions, was being held up"* in order that one SDA medic could finish reading his Bible.

This risky mission did not go well, and the hill was covered with the bodies of wounded and dead American soldiers. Doss was the only one standing there alone. After lowering the first wounded man, Doss realized that the task was moving too slowly, so he improvised a double knot rope sling, which he used to lower the rest of the wounded men.

 There was no time to count the wounded. His superior estimated the number at 100, but Doss thought it must have been no more than fifty, consequently they split the difference and the official number was reported as 75.

---

[43] Ibid., 118.

Captain Tann looked at Doss' uniform, which was stiff and covered with dried blood and decided that it was time to outfit this brave medic with a new uniform. Thus ended Doss' most remarkable day of rest. He was nominated for two Purple Hearts, but Doss said that one was enough.

Desmond Doss Last Patrol

On his last patrol with his company, a Japanese soldier threw a grenade that landed by his feet. He put his foot on top of the grenade, which exploded. At that moment another soldier called for help. Doss responded in spite of his wounds, and as he crawled towards the wounded soldier, he felt he was about to pass out. He lay down with his head downhill until he recovered, and then proceeded on his mission. He had to repeat this maneuver to avoid a blackout.

 He took care of the soldier's wounds and then tried to do the same with his own. He was bleeding profusely. He blacked out with his feet sticking out of a hole. The first thing he noticed was an unexploded artillery shell a few inches from his head. His comrades located him, put him on a litter, but there was another soldier with a head wound. He insisted that they take him first, since a head wound took precedence over a body wound. Before he was rescued, another bullet lodged in his arm. When he regained consciousness, he was on a hospital ship on his way to Guam.

President Truman's Greatest Honor

From Guam Doss was transferred to the United States where he met his wife after two years of separation. It was October 1945, and the war was over. He soon learned that he was scheduled to be awarded the Congressional Medal of Honor, together with a selected group of sixteen men entitled to the highest honor the grateful country could bestow on those who had excelled in their bravery during the long protracted war. When his turn came, President Truman held Doss' hand while the following citation was read:

"Private First Class Desmond T. Doss was a company aid man with the 307th Infantry Medical Detachment when the 1st Battalion of that

regiment assaulted a jagged encampment 400 feet high near Orasoo-Mura, Okinawa, Ryukyu Islands, on April 29, 1945.

As our troops gained the summit, a heavy concentration of artillery, mortar, and machine-gun fire crashed into them, inflicting approximately seventy-five casualties and driving the others back.

Private Doss refused to seek cover and remained in the fire-swept area with the many stricken, carrying them one by one to the edge of the encampment and there lowering them on a rope-supported litter down the face of a cliff to friendly hands.

On May 5, he unhesitatingly braved enemy shelling and small arms fire to assist an artillery officer. He applied bandages, moved his patient to a spot that offered protection from enemy fire; and, while artillery and mortar shells fell close by, painstakingly administered plasma.

Later that day, when an American was severely wounded by fire from a cave, Private Doss crawled to him where he had fallen twenty-five feet from the enemy position; rendered aid; and carried him 100 yards to safety while continually exposed to flying bullets.

The trio was caught in the enemy tank attack and Private Doss, seeing a more critically wounded man nearby, crawled off the litter and directed the bearers to give their first attention to the other man.

Awaiting the litter bearer's return, he was again struck, this time suffering a compound fracture of one arm. With magnificent fortitude he bound a rifle stock to his shattered arm as a splint and then crawled 300 yards over rough terrain to the aid station.

On May 21, in a night attack on high ground near Shuri, he remained in exposed territory while the rest of his company took cover, fearlessly risking the chance that he would be mistaken for an infiltrating Japanese and giving aid to the injured until he was himself seriously wounded in the legs by the explosion of a grenade.

Rather than call another aid man from cover, he cared for his own injuries and waited hours before litter bearers reached him and started carrying him to cover.

Through his outstanding bravery and unflinching determination in the face of desperately dangerous conditions, Private Doss saved the lives of many soldiers. His name became a symbol throughout the 77th Infantry Division for outstanding gallantry far above and beyond the call of duty.

Then President Truman stated the following: *"I am proud of you. You really deserve this. I consider this a greater honor than being President."*[44] Following this ceremony, the War Department issued an even longer press release detailing the incredible service Private Doss had rendered to the country on the battlefields of Guam, Leyte, and Okinawa. Upon his return to his hometown at Lynchburg, he was treated to a hero's welcome and paraded through Main Street.

Days of Peace and Adversity

Soon after the excitement of all the honors he had received, a medical examination revealed that Doss had contracted tuberculosis. The long exposure to humidity, lack of sleep, exhaustion, and lack of proper nutrition had exacted its toll on this brave American soldier. He lost his left lung, and he was spitting blood for days. He was awarded 100 percent disability; but his pension totaled $118 a month, which was insufficient for a family of three. He began door-to-door sales, and his wife performed part-time housecleaning while taking care of their child plus her sister's two children.

In 1957 he was treated by Hollywood and listened with deep interest to the program: *This is Your Life*. At the end of the program in which some of his military officers participated, he was presented with *"a power saw, a power*

---

shop, movie camera, money enough to increase his little holding on Lookout Mountain to seven acres, a cow, a tractor with attachments, and a station wagon."[45] This allowed his wife, Dorothy, to go back to school and get her nursing degree.

Twenty years after Doss received his Medal of Honor, another Seventh-day Adventist soldier who elected not to bear arms was awarded a Bronze Star medal of honor for his bravery in Vietnam. His name was Curtis A. Reed, of Gillete, Wyoming. Thanks to the bravery of Desmond T. Doss, Reed's reception and treatment in the army was radically different from the one Doss had originally encountered. There was no ridicule for him, nor army boots flying over his head. But Reed was not the only beneficiary of the faithful service Doss had rendered to his country. Thousands of Adventists servicemen were the recipients of special concessions and kind treatment since then.

 In 1962, Desmond T. Doss was invited by President Kennedy for a ceremony at the White House commemorating the 100th anniversary of the creation of the Congressional Medal of Honor. Again, the soldier who was almost kicked out of the army for refusing to bear arms because he felt human life was a sacred gift of God; who was almost court-martialed more than once; and who had risked his own life under heavy enemy fire in order to save the life of others; had the rare privilege of meeting with the president of the United States of America. It had not been easy, but the sacrifice was worth the effort.

Desmond T. Doss' respect for the sacredness of human life was determined, persistent, and inflexible in spite of suffering, deprivation, threat to his life, and constant enemy fire. This respect for life was instilled in him since childhood by his parents and the Seventh-day Adventists community that nourished his soul. Of course, all this took place several decades before nine unelected judges determined that the unborn had no inherent right to life, and could therefore become the target of those who had been the participants of the sexual liberation of the sixties.

---

[45] Ibid., 188.

Desmond Doss Legacy

Doss never issued a public statement about abortion, but given his respect for human life, and his willingness to risk his own life in order to save the lives of others, it might be proper to assume that, had he lived in our time, he would likely be willing to defend the life of the unborn. His heroic life stands as a fit symbol of the Adventist attitude towards the moral value of human life at that time.

In the chapters that follow, the present investigation will hopefully reveal the impact, if any, the moral revolution of the sixties had on the Adventist community's attitude toward the sanctity of human life. Doss had placed the safety of others ahead of his own. Would those who share his faith do likewise in the way they treat those whose lives are at risk? For Doss, the lives of others were worth more than his own. Would those who are nurtured by the same religious beliefs emulate his dedication to the sanctity of human life?

THE GREAT CONTROVERSY

 Seventh-day Adventists are familiar with the *"great controversy"* theme, which for them is a symbol of the great cosmic battle between good and evil, God and Lucifer, also known as Satan; a conflict that allegedly started in heaven and is now raging on planet earth; a struggle that will end with the return of Jesus Christ to this world as King of Kings and Lord of Lords. Ellen G. White chose said phrase as the title for her best-known book, *The Great Controversy.*[46]

In it she described how in the last conflict between the forces of good and evil, God's *"Remnant"* will be persecuted for the crime of worshipping God on the seventh-day of the week in obedience to the Fourth Commandment of the Decalogue. Said persecution, according, to Mrs. White, will be orchestrated by the Catholic Church with the assistance of the civil power, and a death decree will be issued towards those who refuse to accept Sunday, the false day of worship.

Ellen G. White seems to have been obsessed with the issue of Sabbath observance and the predicted persecution of those who would refuse to switch their allegiance to the observance of Sunday as a day of worship. SDA's inherited this obsession from her. A search of her writings using the word Sabbath yielded a 2315 count, while a similar search for the word *"abortion"* yielded zero instances. History may eventually justify this obsession of her, but it may fault her for keeping silence on the abortion issue.[47]

---

[46] Ellen G. White. *The Great Controversy* (Mountain View, California: Pacific Press Publishing Association, 1939).
[47] "Seventh-day Adventist Periodical Index" *Andrews University Library.*
http://www.andrews.edu/library/car/sdapiindex.html

This *"great controversy"* title for this chapter was chosen because the battle between good and evil was fought and is being waged right now not so much about the Sabbath, but rather about the right to life of the unborn, and the death decree has been already issued–it was issued back in 1973– and it is already being implemented; but the victims are not those who worship God on the correct day of the week; they are not among those who refuse to honor Sunday as the "Lord's Day;"

Actually, they are not even able to worship, since they are among those waiting for the privilege of being born; and the instigator of this massacre is not the Catholic Church–actually the Bishop of Rome is in fact the most adamant defender of the innocents–but rather the U.S. Supreme Court.[48]

The Opinions of the Ministry Magazine Readers

The big question is: What role did the SDA church play in this life and death controversy? The best source for this is found in the pages of *Ministry,* the international journal of the Seventh-day Adventist Ministerial Association.

The material for this chapter was selected from the chapter bearing the same title in the first book I published about the topic of abortion. I am including here a very small sample of the comments made by authors and readers of said magazine.

As you read the comments of the readers of *Ministry* you will probably wonder how our church managed to make such a dramatic detour from the original pro-life position espoused by the founders of our church. I encourage you to keep reading, and you will probably find out the answer to this enigmatic question!

---

[48] In the last book of the Bible, *Revelation,* John describes the persecuting activities of a religio-political power symbolized by a predatory beast. Protestants believe that this prediction met its fulfillment first through pagan Rome and later by means of Christian Rome during the Middle Ages through the infamous Catholic Inquisition.

W.R. Beach[49]

> *"It will be tragic, indeed, if our church should support the free and willful destruction of human life (abortion for convenience), while urging those who are of military age not to bear arms in order to refrain from taking life–even that of the enemy."*

The same church [SDA] that encouraged young military draftees to refuse the bearing of arms during WWII as a sign of respect for the sanctity of human life, now argues that Jesus died to preserve our right to *"choose"* to kill when dealing with abortion. The message seems to be: Killing an enemy in self defense is murder, but killing a harmless unborn child is a sacred right.

Chris Harter[50]

> *"Thank you so much! I'm so happy and so proud of Dr. Richard Muller, our church, and Ministry for printing "Abortion: A Moral Issue?" I've been starving for months for some affirmation that abortion is wrong.*
>
> *What are we ministers of God doing if we are not speaking out on moral issues? I wish that at the coming General Conference session we would settle once and for all that life from conception to its natural end should be considered sacred and therefore protected. In the light of eternity our silence may be counted against us on this issue."*

How many anti-abortion sermons have you heard preached by Adventist pastors lately? I haven't heard a single one since my membership transfer four decades ago to the Loma Linda University Church located in Loma Linda,

---

[49] W.R. Beach, "Abortion?" *Ministry* (Mar. 1971): 3-6.
[50] Chris Harter, "Letters" *Ministry* (July 1985): 2.

California. I have heard the same testimony from many pro-life Adventists I know. What does this tell you about our Adventist commitment to the pro-life cause? Do we really care about the merciless slaughter of the unborn and the violation of the Commandment which forbids the shedding of innocent blood?

Robert H. Dunn[51]

> *"It is refreshing to note that Dr. Muller takes the biblical or absolutist position, which defines humanity at the moment of conception, the beginning of life, when the fetus does not "receive a soul" but "becomes a soul" and from then on can be recognized as a living person, a human being with legal and moral rights."*

John Youngberg and Millie Youngberg[52]

> *"We hold that elective abortions violate the fundamentals of any Bible believing community of faith, but is particularly serious to Seventh-day Adventists."*

Kevin Paulson[53]

> *"Adventist doctrine and practice should be based on a plain "Thus said the Lord." And nowhere does Inspiration declare that personhood begins at conception."*

---

[51] Robert H. Dunn, "Letters" *Ministry* (Oct. 1985): 2.
[52] John Youngberg and Millie Youngberg, "The Reborn and the Unborn" *Ministry* (Nov. 1985): 12-13.
[53] Would Kevin Paulson insist on a "thus said the Lord" for condemning genocide, polygamy, and slavery?

This is really hard to understand, because Pastor Kevin Paulson is a highly respected Adventist evangelist whose articles are published even today by conservative publications such as "*Advindicate.*"

Robert E. Hays[54]

> *"I have just read Kevin Paulson's letter in the January 1986 issue of Ministry. To argue for abortion because the Bible doesn't specifically condemn it would be like arguing against the moral law, or the Trinity, or against the use of the word* sacrament, *or against using the word* omniscient *or* omnipresent *to describe God simply because we don't find those specific words in the Bible."*

I was saddened when I read what Kevin Paulson wrote about abortion. I had a hard time believing that an Adventist evangelist of his caliber would show such a disdain for the value of human life—a gift that only God can give. The first time I read an article authored by this man of God, I was impressed by his extensive knowledge and writing ability. His topic was creation, and he did do a marvelous work. Imagine my disappointment when I read his defense of killing innocent unborn children!

Jeremia Florea[55]

> *"Paulson's letter in the January issue of Ministry disturbs me not a little. . . . In the Bible the sixth commandment declares, "Thou shalt not kill." At what age of the fetus does this commandment apply? ... Does the Bible condemn smoking tobacco? Will brother Paulson please explain?"*

---

[54] Robert E. Hays, "Letters" *Ministry* (May 1986): 30.
[55] Robert E. Hays, "Letters" *Ministry* (May 1986): 30.

R. M. Cargill[56]

> *"I want to congratulate John and Millie Youngberg for the article "The Reborn and the Unborn." It is time something be said to lead our thoughts back to the truth of God's Word. It is time to call sin by its right name."*

Thomas Hamilton[57]

> *"According to what I read, the Seventh-day Adventist Church considers it all right to kill an unborn baby if the baby's father was a certain kind of sinner—a rapist or a child molester. It is also considered right to kill an unborn baby if its mother became sexually active when very young. Why should an unborn baby be put to death for its father's or mother's sins?"*

Excellent point! Scripture condemns punishing the children for the sins of their parents.[58]

> New Living Translation
> *"The person who sins is the one who will die. The child will not be punished for the parent's sins, and the parent will not be punished for the child's sins."*

Yes, the Bible is crystal clear on this unmistakable moral concept!

---

[56] R. M. Cargill, "Letters" *Ministry* (Nov. 1986): 28.

[57] Thomas Hamilton, "Letters" *Ministry* (Mar. 1988): 2.

[58] Ezek. 18:20.

William L. Gutel[59]

> *"The greatest moral issue of the past fifteen years is the cold-blooded murder of twenty million babies–and your church says nothing! Could it be that you "strain at a gnat and swallow a camel"? What is more important–saving people from eating meat or saving the lives of innocent babies?"*

Now the number of victims of the abortion genocide has surpassed the 56 million figure. It is high time to put a stop to this atrocious practice—especially among those who still believe in the permanence and validity of the Ten Rules for Human behavior given to us by the Lord. If we did outlaw slavery, why can't we do the same with the killing of the unborn?

When the opportunity to profit from abortion came, the then President of the North American Division argued that there were too many people in the world, and that abortion would alleviate the problem of over population. He said this in the richest country of the world, a country that had a surplus of food. This is very hard for me to understand!

Pauline W. Phillips[60]

> *"God is no respecter of persons. He is impartial. There is no reason in his sight to preserve the life of an adult at the expense of children or the unborn."*

We have the tendency to value human beings on the base of accomplishments, while the Lord has a different way of determining the moral worth of individuals. This is why Jesus identified himself with *"the least of these,"* and I doubt that there is any other group of human beings more qualified to

---

[59] William L. Gutel, "Letters" *Ministry* (Mar. 1988): 2.
[60] Pauline W. Phillips, "Letters" *Ministry* (July 1988): 29.

belong to the least of these group than the unborn. Actually, our eternal destiny will be determined by the way we treat them![61]

Stephen P. Bohr[62]

> *"I would like to thank you for publishing the article by Richard Fredericks, "Less than Human." It is comforting to read such a clear, gutsy, and brilliant article on abortion, especially after reading so many wishy-washy, ambivalent, nonposition rationalizations on the issue. ... I think that we need to take a clear position on the sanctity of all human life."*

The article *"Less than Human,"* written by Richard Fredericks, is one of the best pro-life documents ever authored by an Adventist writer. If you have never read it, I encourage you to do this. Here is the link![63]

Perhaps it is significant to note that Pastor Fredericks is no longer with us. When our church adopted the *"Guidelines on Abortion"* which redefined the true meaning of the Sixth Commandment of the Decalogue, this valiant pro-life Adventist leader left the church and started his own ministry. He is not the only one we lost as a result of our compromise with evil. Several others did the same, and some of them joined the Catholic community of faith because of its firm stand against abortion.

What a shame that such talented Adventist individuals had to leave our community of faith because they could no longer support a church that began to profit from the violation of one of God's Commandment, the one that prohibits the taking of human life. I can relate to their experience. I did also leave the church for three months and worshipped with our Seventh Day

---

[61] Matt. 25:40-45.
[62] Stephen P. Bohr, "Letters" *Ministry* (July 1988): 29.
[63] https://www.ministrymagazine.org/archive/1988/03/less-than-human

Baptists. But I came back because I believe that my Adventist Church may repent of this unfortunate moral detour and ask God for forgiveness.

Andrew Auxt[64]

> *"Thank you, Dr. Fredericks, for your tremendous plea for the lives of the unborn children. I am not an Adventist. I have, however, made considerable effort to meet and talk with Adventists in our area in order to establish a common ground on the basis of mutual faith in the Lord Jesus Christ. It has been a gratifying experience for the most part. One thing that has grieved me is the lack of stand against abortion. ... Some Christian leaders have said that God will have to judge America for its legalization and acceptance of this latter-day holocaust."*

Those who have been blessed with great light, will be held to a higher standard in the Day of Judgment. On that day, many Catholics and Evangelicals will condemn us, because they did honor the right to life granted to all human beings by the Creator, but we did not.

Jeremiah Florea[65]

> *"The well-documented article "Less than Human?" of March 1988 was enlightening but also shocking to us. As Seventh-day Adventists we are sure about the fourth commandment and emphasize it every chance we have. This we should do. But apparently we are not so sure about the meaning of the sixth and first commandments. This is tragic! It appears also that in this area we may have to do some repenting."*

True indeed! The need for repenting is real and urgent. We have a noticeable obsession with the sacredness of the Sabbath—and this is commendable;

---

[64] Andrew Auxt, "Letters" *Ministry* (July 1988): 30.
[65] Jeremiah Florea, "Letters" *Ministry* (July 1988): 30.

nevertheless, isn't life as valuable as sacred time? Didn't Jesus say that the Sabbath was made for man and not the reverse?

 A few years ago, when I was working on my doctoral dissertation, one day I decided to visit the Loma Linda University Library's *"Heritage Room."* I was looking for material which had been published in our Adventist periodicals dealing with the issue of abortion. I was appalled by the scarcity of articles that had been published in recent years. Then it occurred to me to check the number of articles that had been published during the same time span on the Sabbath. I was shocked.

Here is the result: I counted 242 articles dealing with the issue of abortion listed in our Adventist Periodical Index between 1971 and 2006. Now compare this with the number of articles dealing with our favorite subject, the Sabbath. I located 21,324 articles dealing with said topic for the 1971-2006 years in our Periodical Index, which means that for every topic dealing with abortion we published 88 topics on the Sabbath.

This fact seems to suggest that for us the most important subject is sacred time; human life is not. Evidently, our focus lately has been on the sacredness of holy time, while neglecting the importance of the sacredness of human life.

Glen L. Wiltse[66]

"I say amen to Richard Fredericks' article "Less than Human?" in the March issue. For far too long we have, as a church, pussyfooted around on the issue of abortion and failed to take a stand. For a church whose beliefs are entirely based on the Bible and nothing but the Bible, the issue seems patently clear—abortion is murder and should be clearly recognized as such. The risk of loosing some popularity with the majority and loosing some of the business in our medical facilities are not reasons enough to renege on an issue that has such a humane and Christian answer."

---

[66] Glen L. Wiltse, "Letters" *Ministry* (July 1988): 30.

J. David Newman[67]

> *"Our articles on abortion have touched a sensitive nerve. We are receiving more email on this subject than on any other recently published article. The letters are running 10 to 1 in favor of the church adopting a stricter standard.The* Adventist Society of Abortion Education *is a nonprofit group dedicated to educating the general public (Adventists in particular) about the injustice of abortion and about abortion alternatives. ... For further information, contact Teresa Beem, ASAE, P.O. Box 82, Keene, TX"*

If there was so much interest about the abortion issue, you may wonder what happened to change this. The answer is rather simple: The leadership of the church adopted a pro-choice/pro abortion attitude toward killing the unborn.

I must note that Teresa Beem left the Adventist Church with her husband and is now worshipping with our Catholic brethren who have not compromised on abortion issue. Rome may be wrong on the state of the dead and on several other doctrinal beliefs, but it is definitely correct on the state of the living! We must give credit where credit is due! The Catholic Church has stood firm in defense of the right to life of the unborn in spite of the worldwide embrace of the notion that choice truncates morality and justice.

Ken Blake[68]

> *"I commend Ministry for . . . listing the abortion guidelines voted by General Conference officers in 1971 for Adventist medical institutions. However well intentioned, the guidelines unfortunately are flawed with euphemisms, vagueness, and lack of logic.*

[67] J. David Newman, "First Glance" *Ministry* (July 1988): 3.
[68] Ken Blake, "Letters" *Ministry* (May 1988): 2, 27.

For the pregnant woman who is not ready to be a mother, the abortion decision is not an easy one; nevertheless, God's command is crystal clear: *"You shall not murder,"* and murder is defined as the killing of an innocent human being!

Abortion does not solve the moral problem. Actually it compounds it. The woman will have to struggle with a guilty conscience for the rest of her life. She may experience a temporary relief, but the guilt feeling will never completely subside and disappear.

George Gainer[69]

> *"When I first heard and then confirmed that the hospitals of the Adventist Health System in North America were "performing hundreds of abortions" each year, my response was stunned disbelief. I was certain that the hospitals and physicians involved must be acting outside General Conference policy guidelines. I was wrong. Criterion No. five of the 1971 guidelines states that abortion is acceptable "when for some reason the requirements of functional human life demand the sacrifice of the lesser potential human life.*

> *Criterion No. five's "some reason" not only rendered superfluous the first four guidelines, and the principles on which they are based, but it tragically opened the door to elective abortion (i.e., on demand) in Adventist hospitals two years before the United States Supreme Court Roe v. Wade decision. ... The time has come to change the guidelines."*

---

[69] George Gainer, "Letters" *Ministry* (May 1988): 27.

> *The simple "impairment of health" qualification could be used to justify abortion for a woman who is experiencing depression because she is pregnant again or who is so under less-than-ideal circumstances. It will take the wisdom of Solomon to decide cases such as those involving rape, incest, or the very young. The guilt of infanticide is hardly easier to bear for the young than the sordid crimes that cause their pregnancies."*

 I second this proposal; nevertheless, what is needed is not an alteration of our Guidelines on Abortion, but rather the trashing of said document. Said guidelines were created to justify the killing of unborn children. If we stop the murder of the unborn, the need for such guidelines will disappear. Southern Baptists and Catholics do not have guidelines on abortion—they simply do not do them!

What led us into this moral trap was the financial profit from the violation of God's dictum which forbids the taking of innocent human life. Jesus told us that we cannot serve two Masters. We need to serve either God or Money. The love of money and the fear of the loss of revenue was what blinded our eyes to this undeniable biblical truth. Nevertheless, it it not too late to retrace our steps and rectify what went wrong. The Bible demands this from his chosen people. If we don't, God's judgments will fall on our church and our nation.

Samuelle Bacchiocchi[70]

> *"Like much contemporary thought on this subject, we seem to be concerned to define when in the prenatal or postnatal development embryonic life becomes human and thus entitled to the protection of law."*

---

[70] Samuelle Bacchiocchi, "Letters" *Ministry* (May 1988): 28.

True! We need to have a clear vision about the beginning of human life. Without this knowledge, it is impossible to offer the protection human life is entitled to.

> *"This concern is foreign to biblical thought, where the sanctity of life derives not from the size or the stage of development of the embryo but from the divine gift of life manifested from its conception."*

 I am in perfect agreement with Dr. Bacchiocchi on this. Can we claim that the moral value of Jesus, John the Baptist, or any of the other saints mentioned in the Bible was less in the early stages of development prior to their birth? Can we see the future with clarity? We can't!

This means that we should not play God. God is seated on his throne, and we should not usurp his power and prerogative. We have no right to interfere nor destroy the human lives God is creating in the womb. Once a new life has been created and has started developing, we are precluded from destroying it.

Charles W. Nichols[71]

> *"The Adventist hospital in our metropolitan area has an excellent reputation for patient care and welfare. I was therefore shocked to see in the church's Guidelines on Abortion the low view Adventist have of human life. The 1971 guidelines permit abortion when the child is likely to be born physically deformed or mentally retarded. Does "likely" mean that those who make the diagnosis could be wrong? That statement sends a loud and clear signal to all physically deformed and mentally retarded people that the Adventists regard them as undesirable and not worthy to live."*

---

[71] Charles W. Nichols, "Letters" *Ministry* (May 1988): 28.

Keith Peachey[72]

> *"I have noticed a common inconsistency in your statements concerning abortion. If an unborn fetus is a human being, why should being the result of an immoral act or being handicapped, to whatever degree, be considered worthy of the death sentence? Giving birth to these children might be traumatic to the mother, but abortion could also be considered traumatic to the fetus."*

Joseph L. Story[73]

> *"I am much saddened by George Gainer's article on abortion (August 1991). It is not pleasant to note that for 20 years the overarching ethic that determines policy for our health-care institutions is money. As a health-care worker I have worked in a Catholic hospital. Their stand on abortion has been firm all along.*
>
> *They are not going under because of their stand on abortion. Long ago the servant of the Lord wrote, "The greatest want of the world is the want of men–men who will not be bought or sold." (Education p. 57) . . . Surely, as a church we carry a heavy load of guilt for our participation in abortion on demand."*

In the Day of Judgment, Catholics will condemn us Adventists, because they did not yield to the temptation to compromise with evil on the abortion issue, while we did, ant thus violated the core of our mission to the world.

We started with the premise that we recognized the validity and permanence of God's Commandments, but ended by negating the crystal clear meaning of the Sixth one which forbids murder.

---

[72] Keith Peachey, "Letters" *Ministry* (May 1988): 28.
[73] Joseph L. Story, "Letters" *Ministry* (Apr. 1992): 2.

Richard Fredericks[74]

> *"Dr. Gerald Winslow's article on abortion (May 1988) presents many biblical principles (often with great skill and clarity), but offers as its bottom line and decisive principle a total unbiblical ultimate of "personal autonomy.*
>
> *His definitions and application of grace and freedom are distortions. These biblical terms do not defend personal autonomy, but condemn it, ... God's grace never covers willful, cherished sin, and autonomy is the primordial sin. Autonomy literally means "self-law"– the sinful desire to be one's own ultimate authority."*

 Excellent point! The first to seek autonomy was Lucifer, and Adam and Eve made the same mistake. What a tragedy. Autonomy implies self determination on moral issues. We were granted freedom to choose, but the Lord warned our first parents about the serious consequences of departure from the right path, and we are suffering the tragic result of their wrong choice.

We were made not for autonomy, but rather for faithful obedience to the laws set for our protection.; therefore let us lean on his wisdom and understanding. He knows a little bit more than any of us about what is better for us.

We are blind to the consequences of our moral actions, but the one who created us can see the future with unusual clarity and he wants the best for us. Why should we choose death for us or for our children? Notice what the Bible says about the right choice: [75]

---

[74] Richard Fredericks, "Letters" *Ministry* (Sept. 1988): 26.
[75] Deut. 30:19.

> New International Version
> "This day I call the heavens and the earth as witnesses against you that I have set before you life and death, blessings and curses. Now choose life, so that you and your children may live."

Timothy Jessen[76]

> "It does not surprise when a liberal mainline denomination like my own advocates a policy against life, but the Adventists–the paragon of healthcare, concern for others, adherence to the Scriptures? What about "Thou shalt not kill?""

This adherence to Scripture is no longer practiced by our Adventist Church. It became obsolete the moment abortion on demand was allowed in our own hospitals in a direct violation of the Sixth Commandment of the Decalogue!

R. F. Westendorf[77]

> "The child conceived in adultery is not guilty of that sin. That child should not die so that the woman may escape the consequences of her sin. Any appeal to justice must certainly favor the one who cannot defend himself. I have noticed a common inconsistency in your statements concerning abortion. If an unborn fetuss is a human being, why should being the result of an immoral act or being handicapped, to whatever degree, be considered worthy of the death sentence? Giving birth to these children might be traumatic to the mother, but abortion could also be considered traumatic to the fetus."

---

[76] Timothy Jessen, "Letters" *Ministry* (Sept. 1988): 26.
[77] R. F. Westendorf, "Letters" *Ministry* (Sept. 1988): 26-27.

It seems to me that Westendorf is right! Where is the justice of condemning to death the innocent unborn baby for the sins of the father?

Anonimous[78]

> *"I know a person who is not a victim but the product of rape. This person is a child of God, a Seventh-day Adventist Christian. I wonder how this person feels, thinking that it was God's will that he should have been aborted? . . . I think the Devil has pulled a fast one on us ethical Christians. Abortion has become our Achilles heel."*

 Yes, the Devil set a clever trap for us, and like Eve, we chose to believe his devilish charms. Nevertheless, if we repent of this great error, if we confess our sin and turn away from our evil ways, the Lord will forgive us and set us again on the right path. If we wait, we may discover that the Lord may have to say to us: *"Depart from me, all ye workers of iniquity."*[79]

Dennis Fortin[80]

> *"I can't but think of Mary. Still a teenager, not married, very poor, she declared she was pregnant by the Holy Spirit. What we would do with such a case today in our society that has become so permissive about the sacredness of life? Would we find her guilty of teenage sexual promiscuity? Would we diagnose her a schizophrenic with religious delirium? Would we find her too young, too immature, too poor, to raise a child properly?*

---

[78] "Letters" *Ministry* (Sept. 1988): 27.
[79] Luke 13:27.
[80] Dennis Fortin, "Letters" *Ministry* (Sept. 1988): 27.

> *If because of her situation society told her to get an abortion, would we as a church remain silent? Could this abortion be carried out in an Adventist hospital? Could Christ, our Lord, be born in the cities of America?"*

True! Mary, the mother of Jesus, was lucky that she was not taken care of at our Washington Adventist Hospital, for example, an Adventist medical institution described by a General Conference representative as an *"abortion mill."*

Willard D. Regester[81]

> *"As a physician who has been (I am sorry to say) actively involved on both sides of the abortion question, I am puzzled, baffled, and finally incensed about our church's unwillingness to come to grips with the abortion question and take a stand."*

It is interesting to notice that today many Adventist health care workers tend to avoid the word *"murder"* and opt for euphemisms like *"pregnancy interruption,"* or *"pregnancy termination."* The Adventist Church did listen to Regester and took a stand—a stand on the wrong side of the abortion issue!

Terry C. Grimm[82]

> *"We, as a church, take the stand that it is wrong to take another's life. For this reason we strongly urge our young people to stay out of the military. We base this position on the commandment that states, "Thou shalt not kill.*

---

[81] Willard D. Regester, "Letters" *Ministry* (Nov. 1988): 2.
[82] Terry C. Grimm, "Letters" *Ministry* (Nov. 1988): 30.

> *Yet we don't seem to apply this same commandment when it comes to abortion. Isn't it strange that we can see clearly the application of this commandment to those already born but not see how it could possibly apply to the unborn?"*

Hugo Meier[83]

> *"I read the preliminary Seventh-day Adventist statement on abortion (July 1990) and don't think much of the document. It is very weak. . . . Our institutions should be at the forefront of institutions that refuse to kill the unborn. Guidelines will be subject only to the economic concerns of doctors who perform life-terminating procedures in our institutions."*

 This is reminiscent of the parable of the two sons of the farmer who asked one of them to work in his vineyard, and he said "Yes, I will go," but didn't go; while the other one said "No," but changed his mind and did go to work in his father's vineyard.

We Adventists started by having a great respect for God's Commandment, but then, when the test time came, we ended by compromising on the one forbidding murder; while Rome, who had shown disregard for God's Sabbath ended by standing firm against the killing of innocent human beings.

Can we be humble enough and admit that in this we have erred from the straight path? How can we continue defending the genocide of a large segment of the human population with a straight face?

---

[83] Hugo Meier, "Letters" *Ministry* (Nov. 1990): 29.

Van Ottey[84]

> *"When physical or mental health takes precedence over life, our priorities are out of order. When the fetus's not measuring up to our standards of perfection is grounds for taking its life, our priorities are out of order. When the circumstances of conception (rape or incest) are the determining factor, our priorities are out of order. When it comes to life-or-life situation, then and then only with much prayer abortion should be considered. Jesus said, "Father, if it be possible, let this cup pass from me: nevertheless not as I will, but as thou wilt." We say, "Father, please remove this cup from me. If you don't, then I will.""*

R. W. O'Ffill[85]

> *"It seems unbelievable to me that one person should be able to decide whether another living person shall continue to live or die. To my knowledge, our criminal justice system never gives the decision on capital punishment to one person."*

 This is so true! When a criminal is imposed the death penalty, there is an immediate appeal, and quite often the execution—if ever—is delayed up to 20 years or more. In the case of abortion, the victim is killed no sooner the woman asks for it. No appeals, and no delays! Neither the father nor any of the relatives of the victim have the right to object. In a criminal case, the verdict of a jury is required, while in an abortion case the life of the victim is at the whim of a mentally depressed woman.

---

[84] Van Ottey, "Letters" *Ministry* (Nov. 1990): 29.
[85] R. W. O'Ffill, "Letters" *Ministry* (Nov. 1990): 29.

Sarah Endres[86]

> *"I think that the church should take a strong stand against abortion. And I definitely believe our hospitals should not be allowed to perform abortions. The church's wishy-washy way of dealing with abortions is causing people–in and out of the church–to loose respect for the church."*

Yes! I know of several leading pro-life Adventists who have left our church precisely because of our church compromise with evil on this issue.

David Glenn[87]

> *"I am perplexed about two points in the February 1991 editorial "How Sacred is Human Life?" Point nine seems to indicate that since God has left it with individuals to make choices for God or evil, we, then, have no business to enact laws to protect life."*

Clifford Laurell[88]

> *"I believe the members of the committee should view ultrasonic pictures of a developing human being in the womb. It is this scientific development that led Dr. Bernard Nathanson, an atheist, head of one of the largest abortion clinics, to make the following statement:"I am deeply troubled by my own increasing certainty that I have in fact presided over 60,000 deaths. There is no longer serious doubt in my mind that human life exists within the womb from the very onset of pregnancy.""*

---

[86] Sarah Endres, "Letters" *Ministry* (Feb. 1991): 2.
[87] David Glenn, "Letters" *Ministry* (June 1991): 28.
[88] Clifford Laurell, "Letters" *Ministry* (Aug. 1991): 28.

Ralph Harmon[89]

> *"Have we become so intoxicated by the praise of the world that we want to retain our "good" image even if it means not calling sin sin? I believe we again should let the world know where we stand whether such a stand is popular or not."*

Kenneth B. Blake[90]

> *"I call on all SDA pastors and laypersons who feel strongly that the slaughter of the innocents in our hospitals must end to move as God directs them and to petition current church leaders to repudiate the liberalized abortion guidelines (as amended in 1971), and to reject the Christian View of Human life Committee's draft statement (Ministry, 1990) that would add the pregnancy's adverse effects on a woman's mental health as another justification for abortion."*

Yes, it was the woman's health exception that opened the door for abortion demand in our Adventist medical institutions. This resulted in the deaths of thousands of innocent unborn children in our own medical institutions, children who did nothing to deserve the death penalty.

Leo Schreven[91]

> *"Would an Adventist ordained minister be tempted to leave the "remnant church"? For me the issue of abortion is nearly the cause. My head hangs in shame before all Christian leaders who receive Ministry.*

---

[89] Ralph Harmon, "Letters" *Ministry* (Dec. 1991): 2.
[90] Kenneth B. Blake, "Letters" *Ministry* (Dec. 1991): 2.
[91] Leo Schreven, "Letters" Ministry (Dec. 1991): 27.

> *Are we not the remnant that keep the commandments? Is the sixth commandment less important than the fourth? In evangelism I have lost at least a dozen souls because of this inconsistency. Driving by Adventist hospitals and seeing anti-abortion picketers brings tears to my eyes. Especially [sic] when the Catholic or Baptist hospital down the road is known as a "non-murdering" facility."*

David F. Crawford[92]

> *"Although I do not adhere to Catholic theology, I applaud that [Catholic] church's stand on abortion. I challenge my church leadership to abolish administering abortions in all SDA facilities–at the very minimum, abortion on demand."*

Crawford wrote these words some decades ago, and he is probably still waiting for his wish to take place. I share his desire and pray that it may become a reality. This is precisely why I am writing my second book on this life and death issue.

Jeremiah Florea[93]

> *"Upon reading the articles by Kis and Gainer, I didn't know what to think. Suppose during the past hundred years we had handled the fourth commandment from an economic standpoint, as we appear to be doing with the sixth now, would we have a Seventh-day Adventist Church today?"*

---

[92] David F. Crawford, "Letters" *Ministry* (Dec. 1991): 27.
[93] Jeremiah Florea, "Letters" *Ministry* (Dec. 1991): 27. For more on the same idea, read "Is Abortion Less Offensive to God than Sabbath Breaking?" in Chapter XI of this study.

True! Worshipping God on the correct day of the week is important, but so is respecting the right to life of every human being created or being created in the image of God. Abortion is a direct affront to the Life Giver who sacrificed his lifestyle in heaven that we might have life. How can we in return, sacrifice the life of our own children to protect our lifestyle?

David Miceli[94]

> *"Our church has a moral responsibility to uphold God's law. How can we realistically expect others to take our Sabbath message seriously when we have remained silent on the moral implications of the sixth commandment while millions of unborn children perish in our midst? Is it reasonable to anticipate that the Sabbath commandment, historically the most dispensable of the ten, will some day judge the sixth, arguably the most inviolate of the ten, without somehow having a moral imperative inherent within it?"*

The Deafening Silence After the Storm

 Following the publication of the 1992 amended official version of the *Guidelines on Abortion*, the fierce abortion battle died down within the pages of *Ministry*. These guidelines, together with the publication of the book *"Abortion: Ethical Issues and Options,"* dealt a deathblow to the pro-life movement within the SDA Church, and many of the most militant SDA pro-lifers left the church in order to pursue ministries more akin to their personal moral convictions. At the same time, some of those who were open to the acceptance of a pro-life position by the church, lost no time in consolidating their pro-choice leanings.

---

[94] David Miceli, "Letters" *Ministry* (July 1993): 29.

THE TIME OF TROUBLE

 Seventh-day Adventists are also familiar with the biblical *"time of trouble"* theme, which was amply developed by the most prolific SDA author, pioneer, and prophetic guide of the Adventist movement: Ellen G. White. This time of trouble was originally experienced by Jacob, the ancestor of the Jewish race, when he learned that his brother Esau was coming against him with four hundred armed soldiers evidently with the plan to carry out his desire for revenge for having been cheated by his brother out of his inheritance.

Daniel the prophet described another time of trouble for God's people before their providential liberation,[95] and Ellen White predicted that Seventh-day Adventists would experience this time of trouble when a death decree would be issued against Sabbath-keepers prior to the return of Jesus Christ to this earth to establish his eternal kingdom.

Richard Fredericks, in an article published by *Spectrum* two decades ago, made the following surprising declaration:[96]

> *"Speculation about a future death decree should not make us actively participate in the present one. Surely, for the unborn of America, this is already a time of trouble such as has never been."*

Many pro-life writers have stated that the most dangerous place on earth is not the Middle East, where people were being slaughtered recently by the hundreds, but rather inside the womb, where developing babies are exterminated en mass by the millions for the crime of having not seen yet the light of day. If this is not *"a time of trouble such as has never been,"*[97] then the expression has lost its true meaning.

---

[95] Daniel 12:1.
[96] Richard Fredericks, "A Biblical Response to Abortion" *Spectrum* 19/4 (May 1989): 33..
[97] Daniel 12:1.

A Biblical Response to Abortion

by Richard Fredericks

 Richard Fredericks[98] chose the following title for the article published by Spectrum in 1989: *"A Biblical Response to Abortion."*[99] The material is similar to another document written by him entitled *"A Compassionate and Christian 'Quality of Life' Ethic,"* which was published as one of the chapters of the book edited by David Larson, *"Abortion: Ethical Issues & Options,"*[100] which is summarized in Chapter VIII of my first book dealing with abortion.[101]

Fredericks started his topic with the experience of a nurse who held a strong pro-life attitude towards abortion. When she was in nursing school, one of the course requirements was to participate in an abortion. She refused, and the school allowed her to graduate in spite of her refusal to fulfill that portion of her training.

After graduation, she learned that not only abortions were routinely performed in Adventist hospitals, but that most of them were elective ones. She had a chance to see the pictures of aborted babies and realized that what was being dismembered were not unwanted human tissue, but rather little hands, feet, heads and torso. She learned how one baby that had survived a saline abortion and was alive and crying was placed inside a sealed bucket to suffocate. She thought that this was murder.

This experience prompted Fredericks to investigate the facts connected with abortion, and he learned that the lives of one and a half million unborn babies were routinely destroyed every year in the United States of America, and that

---

[98] Fredericks is a graduate from Andrews University, and he was teaching religion at Columbia Union College at the time of the publication of his article by *Spectrum*.

[99] Fredericks, 29, 33.

[100] David Larson. *Abortion: Ethical Issues & Options* (Loma Linda, California: Center For Christian Bioethics, 1992), xi.

[101] "From Pro-life to Pro Choice"
http://www.lulu.com/shop/search.ep?type=&keyWords=nic+samojluk&sitesearch=lulu.com&q=&x=12&y=12

the *"war on the unborn"* was producing twice the number of casualties every year than the combined death that resulted from all the major American wars, starting with the Civil War and including the Vietnam War.

 Then Fredericks met a woman named Patti McKinney, the president of Women Exploited by Abortion (WEBA), a pro-life organization with 36,000 members with chapters in 30 states. This woman left the SDA church because she felt she didn't want to share in the guilt associated with the killing of the unborn.

She had challenged SDA's with the following question: *"OK, Adventists, what about the sixth commandment?"* Her question was met with apathy, especially by the SDA clergy, in spite of the fact that the Bible condemns the killing of innocent human beings:

The Bible forbids murder, it prohibits the killing of children for the sins of their parents,[102] declares that the Lord hates the shedding of innocent blood,[103] and establishes a link between child sacrifice and materialistic fulfillment and greed.[104]

This link, according to Fredericks, was confirmed by archeologists who discovered that in the city of Carthage wealthy families engaged in the religious practice of sacrificing their children for economic reasons: they were disposing their unwanted children in order to preserve their lifestyle.[105]

Besides, Fredericks cited numerous biblical passages demonstrating that there is nothing to suggest that the unborn is potential instead of actual human life:[106]

"Thus says the Lord, your Redeemer, and the one who formed you in the womb, I, the Lord, am the maker of all things."

---

[102] Deut. 24:16; Jer. 7:30-34; Micah 6:7; Psalms 106:35-40.
[103] Prov. 6:16-17.
[104] Jer. 22:3,13-17.
[105] Biblical Archeological Review (January/February 1984).
[106] Jer. 1:5; Isa. 44:24, 25.

"Abortion is a false Gospel," affirmed Fredericks. It claims redemption through the shedding of innocent blood for the sins of the parents instead of relying on the blood shed by the Son of God. He cited Mother Teresa on the occasion of receiving the Nobel Peace Prize in 1979, and the earliest non-biblical moral code the Didache:[107]

> *"To me, the nations with legalized abortion are the poorest nations. The great destroyer of peace today is the crime against the innocent unborn child. ... In destroying the child, we are destroying love, destroying the image of God in the world."*
>
> *"You will not kill. You will not have sex with other people's spouses. You will not abuse young children. You will not have sex outside of marriage. You will not abort fetuses."*

Then Fredericks reminded his readers that Jesus was born into poverty, hardship, and suffering, which is evidenced by the nativity scene. Had Mary lived in our time, she would have been advised to seek an abortion. She was single, poor, and pregnant. God's glory was revealed in the birth of Jesus in the midst of poverty and deprivation, bereft of the lifestyle we are accustomed to today, thus showing that the *"love of money"* is not the secret of happiness, but rather the *"root of all evil;"* and that *"life does not consist in the abundance of . . . possessions."*[108]

The practice of abortion goes against the true Gospel, argued Fredericks, since most of the abortions are carried out prompted by economic reasons. Jesus did not say *"Blessed are the rich,"* but rather *"Blessed are the poor."* Many argue that women have the right to decide what to do with their own body, forgetting that the Bible says that our bodies are not our own: *"You are not your own; you were bought with a price; therefore, honor God with your body."*[109]

---

[107] Fredericks, 31.
[108] Luke 12:16-21.
[109] 1 Cor. 6:19-20, NIV.

He also suggested that it is often claimed that many of the unborn would be better off dead. Who gave this people their crystal ball? Can humans play God? asked Fredericks. He also stated:[110]

> *"The greatest gospel singer of this century was the illegitimate daughter of a 16-year-old poor, black girl who was raped. Beethoven's family background included a deranged father, a syphilitic mother, a mentally retarded older brother, and a sibling born blind."*

There is no doubt that Planned Parenthood would have advised Ludwig's mother to have an abortion, Fredericks asserted. Given human's inability to foresee the future, should SDA's justify abortion on the basis of personal freedom? God respects personal freedom, no doubt, but there are serious consequences if we misuse said God-given freedom. Some Adventist preachers think that being pro-life may hasten the predicted curtailment of religious freedom for SDAs. Here is Fredericks' response:[111]

> *"Speculation about a future death decree should not make us actively participate in the present one. Surely, for the unborn of America, this is already a time of trouble such as has never been."*

Next, Fredericks related the experience of half a dozen students he had the privilege to counsel. They opted for an abortion for economic reasons because they wanted to finish school and in order to keep their relationship with their boyfriends and parents. The unexpected result was that two of them dropped school; others lost their boyfriends, lost contact with their relatives, or ended with terrible guilt feelings.

---

[110] Fredericks, 33.
[111] Ibid.

In one case a girl would vomit every time she turned the vacuum cleaner or caused her to experience flashbacks of her abortion experience; another girl wrote to Dr. Fredericks apologizing for her frequent absences from his classes because she felt so depressed she had a hard time concentrating and felt she was constantly in hell. Women do have the legal right to kill their unborn babies, but they lack God's approval for such an action. Then Fredericks quoted Dr. John Willke who stated:

> *"It is easier to scrape the baby out of a woman's womb than to scrape the memory of that baby out of her conscience."*

Fredericks also related the story of a girl who repented of her life of sin, enrolled in school only to discover that she was pregnant. Her options were suicide, abortion, dropping out of school, or giving the baby for adoption. She opted for the last choice, but when the baby was born, she changed her mind and decided to keep the baby after all, but lacking any support from her parents, she had to drop school and moved out of her parent home in order to secure public assistance.

And Fredericks ended his article with the anecdote involving an older black Methodist pastor who was asked whether he believed that a sixteen-year-old girl was capable of raising a child. He responded that not even a 26-year-old woman was capable of raising a child alone. That is the reason we have churches. Then the black pastor added that after baptizing a newborn baby born to a young girl, he called an old couple and asked them to raise the baby, adding that he wanted them to raise the baby's mother at the same time.

THE GREAT BATTLE OF ARMAGEDDON

 The Battle of Armageddon is a biblical motif familiar to Adventists. It refers to the final cosmic struggle between the forces of evil against the Kingdom of God on earth. Most Adventists place such battle in the future when in fact those with a little deeper spiritual vision see it actually figuratively taking place in front of our eyes.

It started when the State of Hawaii declared an open season for the slaughter of the unborn back in 1970, a genocide which spread to U.S. mainland when nine unelected Justices of the Court removed the legal protection from a large segment of the human race in 1973.

We must note that this fight against the unborn was supported by the Adventist leadership right from the start—three years before it spread to the rest of the country--- and the main motivation was profit, or fear of loss of revenue. The fear of God went out the window the moment financial profit entered through the door.

There was a loud outcry by those who believed that the unborn had an inalienable right to life equal to those who had been born already, and the struggle between the supporters of this genocide and the pro-life crowd intensified and has never abated. Said battle for the soul of those doomed to execution was fought and is still being fought both within the Adventist community and in the general population.

I am including in this chapter only a small vignette of the material available on this topic. For a fuller treatment of this topic, please secure a copy of the book I published in 2008 entitled *"From Pro-life to Pro-choice: The Dramatic Shift in Seventh-day Adventist's Attitude Toward Abortion."*[112]

---

[112]http://www.lulu.com/shop/search.ep?type=&keyWords=nic+samojluk&sitesearch=lulu.com&q=&x=12&y=12

The Wisdom of Solomon
by George Gainer

Responding to David Larson's call for papers on abortion, George Gainer wrote a pro-life document dealing with abortion entitled *"The Wisdom of Solomon?"* It was presented at the *"Abortion: Ethical Issues and Options"* conference on abortion held in Loma Linda in November, 1988. The total number of documents presented on said occasion was 36, but only sixteen of those were included in the book edited by David Larson bearing the same title as the conference. Gainers submission was not included,[113] but eventually *Spectrum* Magazine published an abridged version of Gainer's article[114] in 1989. For access to the full version of Gainer's article, click on the link provided in the following footnote:[115]

Gainer started his article with the story of a non-Adventist pastor and his wife who were in search of a Christian physician and landed in the office of a Takoma Park, Maryland, Seventh-day Adventist hospital obstetrician who, after confirming the woman's pregnancy, asked the couple: *"Do you want this baby or do you want an abortion?"* The pastor and his wife looked at each other with shock and disbelief. They got up, said *"We are sorry. We must be in the wrong place!"* and walked out.

Responding to a question from his audience in which he related this incidence, the pastor made the following statement: *"I am sorry to tell you that the Seventh-day Adventists are aborting hundreds of babies in their hospitals."* Six months later, a *Washington Adventist Hospital* [WAH] nurse complained to Gainer: *"Some doctors treat us like their own private abortion clinic."* This was confirmed by a *Washington Post* report claiming that 1494 abortions had been performed between 1975 and 1982 at the WAH according to information provided by the SDA hospital. The article was prompted by a pro-life manifestation in front of the Sligo Church and the WAH.

---

[113] Gainer stated to me that the reason his paper was not included is a mystery to him.
[114] George Gainer, ""The Wisdom of Solomon"?" *Spectrum* 19/4 (May 1989): 38-46. Gainer was a religion teacher at the Takoma Academy at the time of the publication of this article.
[115] http://www.scribd.com/doc/160731861/The-Wisdom-of-Solomon-or-The-Politics-of-Pragmatism-The-General-Conference-Abortion-Decision-1970-71

Gainer's investigation into the SDA position on abortion revealed that a great step towards the liberalization of abortion had taken place in Hawaii, following the repeal of the State's abortion laws in 1970. *Castle Memorial Hospital* [CMH], a SDA institution, had previously performed therapeutic abortions when pregnancy was the result of rape, incest, or when there was a threat to the physical or mental health of the patient.

Shortly after the repeal of the abortion prohibition was passed by the State of Hawaii, a man who had donated $25,000 for the construction of the hospital came demanding that the hospital perform an elective abortion for his 16-year-old daughter. He produced the copy of a brochure that read as follows: *"This hospital will be a full service hospital and will provide every service that is needed by the residents of the community."*

The hospital administrator contacted the office of the Pacific Union, and the query eventually reached the General Conference in Washington. It was discovered that the SDA church had no official position on the abortion issue, and the hospital decided to issue a temporary ruling allowing elective abortions during the first trimester of pregnancy.

 Soon after the General Conference officers appointed a committee to study the abortion issue, and on March 17, 1970, Neal C. Wilson, the President of the North American Division, made a public statement announcing that the church would neither promote nor support the legalization of abortion, with the following clarification:

"Though we walk the fence, SDA's lean towards abortion rather than against it. Because we realize we are confronted with big problems of hunger and over-population, we do not oppose family planning and appropriate endeavors to control population."

If this had been uttered by a Chinese Communist leader, it would had been less controversial, but the president of a conservative denomination in the richest country of the world? If there is hunger and overpopulation, wouldn't it make more sense to kill the jailed hard core criminals instead of the most innocent members of the human race?

On May of the same year the General Conference officers approved the *"Suggestive Guidelines for Therapeutic Abortions,"* but the plan to submit this to a vote by the 1970 General Conference session was dropped. Some felt that the guidelines were not liberal enough, and thought that the right solution was to allow SDA hospitals to provide abortion on demand.

 The pressure came from half a dozen non-Adventists CMH physicians, and the hospital administrator feared that those doctors would likely take their patients to other competing hospitals in the event they were not allowed to perform said abortions on demand at CMH, which would mean a loss of revenue for CMH.

Management also felt that the SDA hospital should align their policies with the wishes of the community–which had contributed approximately one million dollars to the hospital–and the laws of the state. They had one problem, though: the rest of the doctors at the hospital were opposed to the liberalization of the abortion policies, for which reason they finally appealed to the General Conference requesting for a ruling on the matter.

Several committees studied the problem and much confusion ensued. The result was that during the rest of 1970 and 1971 two divergent versions of the *Guidelines on Abortion* were circulating, and each hospital was allowed to interpret those guidelines at wish, which allowed CMH to offer abortion on demand.

The stricter version of the guidelines was used for public consumption, and the liberalized version for the use of the SDA hospitals. *"Not until 1986 did any church publication print for church members the more permissive 1971 guidelines."* After citing several pro-life quotations on abortion by SDA pioneers such as James White, J.N. Andrews, and John Henry Kellogg,[116] George Gainer ended his article with the following comment:

---

[116] See Chapter entitled "The Way we Were" of this study for details of the SDA pioneers attitude towards abortion.

> *"The difference in the position on abortion between the founders of Adventism and our present policy, and the difference, all too often, between our policy and actual practice in our Adventist hospitals understandably leads to a rising concern among a growing number of Adventists. Should a church that claims to "keep the commandments of God and have the faith of Jesus" continue to remain confused or even neutral about abortion? Perhaps a sign carried by a protester in front of Sligo Seventh-day Adventist Church on October 5, 1985, sums up the urgency of this issue for the church. It read: "Adventists–Remember the Sixth Commandment too!"*

A Shared Philosophy Regarding Abortion

Population control, the reason given by Neal Wilson, the president of the North American Division of Seventh-day Adventists, for our church involvement with the abortion industry, was evidently shared by a graduate from our Loma Linda University named Edward C. Allred, the man who became one of the most successful abortionists in the history of California.

He became so good at killing unborn children, that he eventually found

himself the owner of over twenty abortion clinics in the state, and to his credit, we must mention that he willingly shared the blood money obtained from his killing business with our Adventist Schools. One of the recipients of this largesse was La Sierra University. This seems quite evident by the fact that there is an *"Edward C. Allred Center"* in the School of Business at said Adventist institution today according to a report published in the Fall 2013 edition of the La Sierra University Magazine.[117]

---

[117] http://advindicate.com/articles/2560

This means that those thousands of aborted babies did not die in vain—some of the profit generated by their deaths is being used to provide a Christian education to Adventist youth. Other Adventist institutions have also benefited by this exceptionally talented businessman. Many abortionists have profited from the abortion business, but he excelled them all.

When he retired, he sold his lucrative business to an Adventist dentist: Irving 'Bud' Feldkamp, whose name was in the news a few years ago when he lost several members of his immediate family in an aiplace crash in a Montana cemetery a short distance from the *"Tomb of the Unborn. ... erected as a dedication to all babies who have died because of abortion."*[118]

The inclusion of abortion clinic magnate Edward Allred in this study is due to several factors: **A.** He joined the SDA church at a young age. **B.** He received a Seventh-day Adventist education, including an M.D. degree from Loma Linda University. **C.** He owned and operated *"Family Planning Associates,"* the largest abortion clinic chain in California.[119]

Christopher Zehnder, pastor of His Nesting Place, located in Downey, California, interviewed Allred live in front of a Christian congregation. Allred admitted that at one time he seriously thought about becoming a SDA minister, but was glad he did not, since it would have proved to be a disaster.

When asked about any guilt feeling for taking the life of so many innocent unborn children, he responded that he was providing a needed service to the community and that all the moral responsibility for the decision to abort was not his but rather that of the pregnant women. He expressed his support for the practice of abortion on the basis of population control, but he acknowledged that most abortions are performed for convenience.

Notice that the same explanation, population control, was allegedly given by Neal Wilson when he was the president of the North American Division of Seventh-day Adventists as the reason for the pro-choice position of the church on the issue of abortion, according to George Gainer.

---

[118] Abortion chain owner's family died in MT cemetery plane crash - near Tomb of the Unborn
[119] Christopher Zehnder, "Edward Allred in the Pulpit" *Los Angeles Lay Catholic Mission* (June 1998).

I still remember that half a century ago, the great scare was communist China with its overpopulation, and the need to stop this population trend somehow.

This uncontrolled population explosion was considered at the time almost as dangerous as the threat of an atomic war. When asked about second trimester abortions, this is how he responded:

> *"Second trimester abortion is ... a much more difficult question than first trimester, both from the standpoint of the difficulty of it, the medical responsibility on the part of the operator for it, and, as far as I'm concerned, from the philosophical. You may say, "Oh no, there's no difference at all between an embryo, 15 seconds after it's fertilized, and a fetus at 24 weeks' gestation." I can't go for that. I think there's a vast difference. A vast difference in every way.*
>
> *But there is a tremendous psychological burden, a moral burden, everything else, on the physician who is involved in late second trimester abortion. I'm not too sure that the Supreme Court did not err in their opinion when they basically gave a carte blanche for second trimester abortion, up to the state of viability."*

Nevertheless, Allred admitted that he performed second trimester abortions, in spite of the fact that he felt it was inappropriate, because if he refused to do so, women would seek such service elsewhere.

He also stated that he hoped that one day the morning-after pills would make it unnecessary for women to seek abortions anymore; and if that would take place, he wouldn't mind if his abortion services would no longer be needed.

In connection with Dr. Allred's relationship with the SDA church, Daniel Nichols had this to say in a Catholic web site:[120]

---

[120] Daniel Nichols, "When I read about Jesus being rejected" *Open Book* (13 Nov. 2005). http://amywelborn.typepad.com/openbook/2005/11/when_i_read_abo.html.

> *"And note that the Seventh Day Adventist teaching hospitals have been in the forefront of developing abortion techniques; some of the most infamous abortionists have been SDA [California's Allred, for example]. Years ago I was denouncing this to an SDA friend, a kindly old man who ran the local health food store. He was sad that his faith's hospitals did abortions, considered it a sort of apostasy. "Yes, and not only that", he said, "Many of them actually serve coffee!" I mean, abortion is bad, but coffee!"*

The fact that Adventist media has been silent on the honors bestowed by La Sierra University on one of the most proficient serial killers of unborn babies is rather significant. *"Advindicate"* is probably the only exception to this Adventist apathy towards the plight of the unborn. For some reason we have developed a blind spot towards the systematic slaughter of those who are waiting for the chance to take their first breath. Notice what the good book says about this:[121]

> *"Rescue those being led away to death; hold back those staggering toward slaughter. If you say, 'But we knew nothing about this,' does not he who weighs the heart perceive it? Does not he who guards your life know it? Will he not repay everyone according to what they have done?"*

Kevin Paulson's Defense of Abortion

Some years ago, I received from Pastor Kevin Paulson a long article written in defense of abortion. I did write a response to some of the ideas contained therein and sent it to him; he answered back saying that he would respond when he could spare the time. Many years have gone by, and I am still

---

[121] Prov. 24:11-12

waiting for his answer. A Google search revealed that his article is online as well, which you can read.[122] Here are some of the arguments that were selected from said article followed by my comments:

"To begin with, Seventh-day Adventists have a time-tested heritage of adhering strictly to the Bible in matters of faith and morality."

 This statement by Paulson sounds rather deceptive. How can anyone defend the killing of innocent human beings and claim that such practice is supported by the teachings contained in Scripture? Can't this man of the cloth read the Sixth Commandment of the Decalogue written by God's finger twice on tablets of stone? Can't he also read our own *Guidelines on Abortion* where it is stated that the Adventist Church does not condone abortions on demand?

"It was Christ who condemned the ancient Jews for "teaching for doctrines the commandments of men"

When did the Sixth Commandment become a human doctrine? Was it Moses or God himself the one who thundered from Mount Sinai: *"You shall not murder"*?

This argument has no foundation on truth. If you compare our Adventist version of the Sixth Commandment with what the Lord wrote on tablets of stone, you will immediately see the contrast.

Our *"Guidelines on Abortion"* are the ones deserving to be labeled as human doctrines based on tradition. How can Paulson claim the opposite with a straight face? And how can our leadership at the General Conference fail to see the white elephant in the room?

---

[122]http://www.adventistlaymen.com/Documents/SEVENTH-DAY%20ADVENTISTS%20AND%20THE%20ABORTION%20QUESTION.htm

> *"Yet the laws he gave to Israel under divine inspiration say nothing specific about it--despite a host of very specific injunctions about murder, manslaughter, and sexual behavior."*

You have it right in front of your eyes, Pastor Paulson, yet you can't see it? Can't you see that murder is the intentional and malicious killing of an innocent human being? The unborn bears all the markers of humanity. It is not an appendix of the pregnant woman; an appendix does not possess human feet, human extremities, its own human heart, and it own human DNA!

> *"Among the Adventist pioneers, J.N. Andrews and John Harvey Kellogg wrote against abortion (6), yet the writings of Ellen White maintain the silence of Scripture on the subject."*

It is true that Ellen White did not use the term "abortion " in her writings; nevertheless, she did refer to the *"almost"* murder of the unborn. Read the following quote from her writings:[123]

> *"If the father would become acquainted with physical law, he might better understand his obligations and responsibilities. He would see that he had been guilty of almost murdering his children, by suffering so many burdens to come upon the mother, compelling her to labor beyond her strength before their birth, in order to obtain means to leave for them."*

---

[123] Selected Messages, Vol. 2 (Washington, D.C.: Review and Herald Publishing Association, 1958), 429-430.

If neglecting the health of a pregnant woman was almost murdering the unborn, can we conclude that Ellen was neutral regarding the actual killing of an unborn baby?

Suppose Ellen could come back to life and we asked her about the above quoted *"almost murdering his children"* statement. Do you think that she would say, *"Sure I was against the almost murder of unborn babies, but I was never against the actual murder of them"?* Would such an answer make any logical sense?

After I discovered this statement by her against the almost killing of the unborn I did share this finding with a leading Loma Linda University ethicist and theologian and this was his immediate reaction: *"This does it! We can no longer argue that Ellen White was silent on abortion."*

Of course, we could add many other statements by Mrs. White where she makes reference to the violation of the Sixth Commandment. Here is one of them:[124]

> *"All acts of injustice that tend to shorten life . . . or any passion that leads to injurious acts towards others, or causes us even to wish them harm . . . all these are, to a greater or less degree, violations of the sixth commandment."*

If, according to the opinion of Ellen White, all harm done to others is a violation of the sixth commandment, how can Paulson conclude that the ultimate form of harm—execution by dismemberment or poison, be excluded from what God prohibited in said rule of human behavior?

> *"Why do so few of them find fault with capital punishment--a flawed system that is often racially biased?"*

---

[124] White. Patriarchs and Prophets *(Washington, D.C.: Review and Herald Publishing Association, 1958), 316.*

What does capital punishment have to do, Pastor Paulson, with abortion? How can you equate the killing of a criminal with the execution of an innocent unborn baby? Besides, on what basis do you argue that the pro-life effort is racially biased? Are you perhaps ignoring the historical origin of the abortion movement? Have you noticed that most abortion clinics are located in ethnic neighborhoods? Are you familiar with the role played by Margaret Sanger and her eugenic program? Wasn't her effort designed to control the growth of the black population?

> *"But the gravest of all their inconsistencies is the refusal to advocate murder charges for women who procure abortions."*

Suppose society decided to press charges against women who have had an abortion, who would volunteer to act as a prosecuting witness? Will the abortionist volunteer? How about the man responsible for her pregnancy? Besides, isn't the pregnant woman a victim of those who take advantage of her weakness? The moment she realizes she is pregnant, her boyfriend, her family and society put pressure on her to seek an abortion.

If she says that she wants to keep her baby, she knows that she must fend for herself, and all her support system vanishes into thin air. If we want to punish the real culprits, we should vent our anger towards those who benefit the most of the murder of the unborn: the impregnator and the abortionist.

> *"Nonmarital sex is in most cases the cause of the abortion dilemma."*

Precisely! It is no mere coincidence that the sexual revolution of the 60's was followed by the legalization of the killing of the unborn in the 70's. Those two events are connected one to the other like conjoined twins. No wonder God placed the prohibition against adultery and fornication next to the injunction against murder in the Decalogue. Sin has a gregarious nature; one sin prepares the way for another. One sin opens the door wide for another one associated with it.

> *"Modern technology, with its new methods of contraception, has made it increasingly difficult for society to "shame" sexually active young people"*

No doubt! This reminds me of what an Adventist parent told her teenage daughter. *"If you get pregnant, remember that there is the abortion alternative;"* and what President Obama said when questioned about his views about abortion: *"I don't want my daughters to be punished with a baby."* Notice what the Bible says about children:[125]

> *"Children are a heritage from the LORD, offspring a reward from him."*

What a contrast between the opinion of God and that of men. God considers children to be a blessing, while men think that pregnancy is a punishment. Some defenders of abortion have gone so far as labeling pregnancy as a disease. This is the reason Planned Parenthood, the largest provider of abortion in the world, describes the killing of unborn children as an integral part of their health services to women. No wonder the government doles half a billion dollars annually to said organization with the pretext that abortion is a valid component of health.

> *"How tragic that the same Christians who deny the claims of God's law and the ability of converted Christians to obey it are the same ones who apparently think civil coercion will succeed where spiritual persuasion has failed."*

I believe, Pastor Paulson, that you are forgetting the proper role of the church and that of the government. The State wields the power of the physical sword, while the church is the guardian of the sword of the Spirit—the Bible. The church is responsible for the spiritual well being of its parishioners,

---

[125] Psalms 127:3

93

while the government's duty is the protection of the assets and life of the human beings under its jurisdiction.

When the life of someone is threatened by a criminal, we do not call the pastor but rather the policeman, and we hope that the one sent can shoot straight. Here is where the government has failed: If the threatened victim is the unborn, the government will protect the one who is about to murder the victim. This type of behavior is an example of the most atrocious dereliction of duty, and when the church sides with the government, it becomes an accomplice to the murder of the unborn.

> *"Through "having a form of godliness, but denying the power thereof" (II Tim. 3:5), she has made coercion a substitute for conversion."*

Pastor Paulson, this statement reveals how far you have departed from a *"thus said the Lord"* on this particular issue. I have read your erudite comments on other issues, and I was impressed. Your knowledge about the Bible and the inspired writings of Ellen White is impressive, but your ignorance of the true and crystal clear meaning of the Sixth Commandment is unbelievably shortsighted. You seem to have developed a blind spot in your spiritual vision regarding the issue of abortion. The church has no power to force anyone to obey God, but the role of the State includes the protection of the major asset of every human being: Life.

Abortion Answers and Attitudes

by John V. Stevens, Sr.

Perhaps the strongest defense of the practice of abortion by a SDA leader was written by John V. Stevens, Sr., who was occupying the position of Pacific Union Conference Public Affairs/Religious Liberty Director at the time of publication of his article entitled *"Abortion Answers and Attitudes"* by the *Pacific Union Recorder* in 1990.[126] Here are some of the arguments he advanced to justify the killing of the unborn, followed by my personal comments:

> *"The best example is Christ who chose to die in order to restore that freedom lost through sin so that all can choose to mold their own destiny. Christ valued choice over life."*

Pro-lifers would ask: "Did Jesus die to make us free to sin or to be free from sin?" To the woman caught in adultery Jesus said: "Neither do I condemn thee. Go and sin no more."[127]

> *"Every human being, created in the image of God, is endowed with a power akin to the Creator—individuality, power to think and to do. (Education, page 17) This takes place after birth, when the developing baby becomes a person."*

The image of God is more than *"the power to think and to do."* It is the power to do God's will. The Devil possesses the power to think and to do in a great measure, but the image of God in him has been distorted because he has lost the power to do God's will. We could say the same about Hitler, Idi Amin, and Bin Laden.

God is described in the Bible as love. This is God's main characteristic. God's image includes the ability to think, to do God's will, and to love. God's love prompted him to give his life in order to save others; those who choose abortion sacrifice the life of the innocent for their own convenience. The contrast is unmistakable! Jesus came down from heaven that we might live; we kill to protect our selfish lifestyle!

---

[126] John V, Stevens, Sr. "Abortion Answers and Attitudes," Pacific Union Recorder (20 Aug. 1990): 12-13.
[127] John 8:11

> *"Pregnancy, abortion, birth, life and death, can all be traumatic. Others have no authority over our consciences in regard to our response to life crucial events. The Holy Spirit is the only True Guardian of the conscience. To allow society–or the state–or the church–or even the family– to replace the Holy Spirit is to be guided by the spirit of the anti-Christ."*

Stevens, with one stroke of his pen, has invalidated and negated the role God has assigned to both the church and the state. If the Holy Spirit has no need of the church or the state, then perhaps we might as well close all our churches and all governments and save some money in the process. Would Paulson apply the same insane principle to other sins of lesser consequence like burglary, the sexual abuse of children, and to rape?

> *"From the perspective of respect for God's Word, Biblical history, and the fundamental principle of free moral agency, the Adventist church could justify adopting a pro-choice position."*

It is interesting to notice the similarity between Stevens' argument justifying abortion and one of the statements included in the official SDA *"Guidelines on Abortion:"*[128]

> *"God gives humanity the freedom of choice, even if it leads to abuse and tragic consequences. His unwillingness to coerce human obedience necessitated the sacrifice of His Son. He requires us to use His gifts in accordance with His will and ultimately will judge their misuse."*

---

[128] Seventh-day Adventist Church. Adventist Beliefs/Guidelines: *Guidelines on Abortion* (12 Oct. 1992).

Perhaps the following question might be in order: Did Jesus die to protect the right of rapists, burglars, and murderers? Did he give his life to secure the rights of women to either poison or dismember their own children? Jesus stated on one occasion: [129]

> *"Whosoever shall offend one of these little ones ... it is better for him that a millstone were hanged about his neck, and he were cast into the sea"*

If offending a little one is such a serious sin against heaven, then how would Jesus have described the murder of one of these little ones? Besides, what is the role of the church? Isn't to warn sinners about the dire consequences of sin and to invite people to repent in order to secure forgiveness? How can preachers like Stevens and Paulson attempt to destroy the basic foundation of their own ministry? If warning women against sin is usurping the role of the Holy Spirit, then Stevens and Paulson are out of a job!

A Reader's Reaction to Stevens Comments

Kathleen Jones sent the following comments to the Editor of the Pacific Union Recorder in response to John V. Stevens', Sr. defense of abortion:[130]

> *"I cannot begin to tell you how horrified I am that a man on the Adventist Church payroll for 20 years, and no doubt receiving retirement benefits, would be so bold as to endorse abortion in a church paper ["Abortion Commandment" by John V. Stevens, Sr., Letters to the Editor, March 2006]. How he can make the nexus between right to life and freedom of worship based on two of the 10 Commandments? "Thou shalt not kill" being the undoing of the right to keep the seventh-day Sabbath is a stretch."*

---

[129] Mark 9:42

[130] Kathleen Jones, "Letters to the Editor" *Pacific Union Recorder* (1 Apr. 2006). http://pauccomm.adventistfaith.org/recorder-archives-pdf

Kathleen Jones was reacting to the following comments made by John V. Stevens, Sr. published in the *Pacific Union Recorder's* section allotted for reader's comments:[131]

> *"Many people view abortion as killing, therefore a Ten Commandments issue. However, nowhere in Scripture are we told that abortion is a crime, or killing, or even a sin. We have been subtly conditioned by religious propaganda from the fundamentalists. The abortion issue is the catalyst that will establish religion in our nation and then everything else will follow."*

For additional arguments advanced by Stevens justifying the killing of the unborn, see Chapter VII of my first book on abortion.[132] He argues that the Bible does not say that abortion is a crime. Pro-lifers would respond that since abortion entails the shedding of innocent blood and the destruction of innocent human life, then it follows that abortion represents a violation of the biblical injunction against murder.

And for a longer list of biblical reasons cited against the practice of abortion, see the argument cited by Richard Fredericks in Chapter V and VIII of my original book entitled *"From Pro-life to Pro Choice"*[133]

---

[131] John V. Stevens, Sr. "Letters to the Editor," *Pacific Union Recorder* (1 Mar. 2006). http://pauccomm.adventistfaith.org/recorder-archives-pdf

[132]http://www.lulu.com/shop/search.ep?type=&keyWords=nic+samojluk&sitesearch=lulu.com&q=&x=12&y=12

[133] Ibid.

THE CALM AFTER THE STORM

 Following the publication of the book edited by David Larson, *Abortion: Ethical Issues & Options* and the official *Guidelines on Abortion* referred to below, an impressive calm ensued about the topic of abortion. SDA publisher's interest in abortion diminished greatly and the number of articles published in SDA magazines dropped dramatically.

An analysis of the content of SDA periodicals published between 1984 and 1993 revealed that there were 144 articles connected either directly or tangentially with abortion. This number dropped to 30 in the following decade. Another discovery revealed that between 1971 and 2006 there were 242 articles listed in the SDA Periodical Index dealing either directly or casually with the word *"abortion,"* while a similar count for the same period indicated a 21,342 count for the term *"Sabbath."*[134] This discovery seemed to indicate that Adventist talk and write about what they consider important. Worshipping on the correct day of the week seems to be important for them, while the genocide of the unborn is not!

 Eventually the great controversy about the abortion seemed to be over among SDA's. Those few pro-lifers who had struggled to stem the liberal tide had fired the last ammunitions they had in their arsenal to no avail. The defenders of women's right to cut short the life of their unborn babies had won. There seemed to be no hope to steer the SDA denominational ship back towards a pro-life haven.

The liberal forces within the denomination had obtained a signal victory for their cause, and some of the most valiant defenders of the rights of the unborn, feeling outnumbered and outgunned, laid their arms and left the SDA

---

[134] "Seventh-day Adventist Periodical Index" *Andrews University.*
http://jewel.andrews.edu:82/search/Xsabbath&SORT=D/Xsabbath&SORT=D&extended=0/3
1993%2C32000%2C32000%2CB/browse

church in order to fight on behalf of the little ones elsewhere. One of them joined the Seventh-day Baptist Church; others started independent ministries; and some went all the way back to Rome and joined the church which has lately been the bastion for the sanctity of the human life from the moment of conception.

SDA Guidelines on Abortion

 The most authoritative official statement about abortion and the sacredness of human life issued by the Seventh-day Adventist organization bears the title *Guidelines on Abortion*,[135] and it was approved and voted by the General Conference of the Seventh-day Adventist Executive Committee at the Annual Council session in Silver Spring, Maryland, on October 12, 1992. This is the date some individual members of the SDA church determined they could no longer be active members of a church that justifies abortion.

Said guidelines is a three-page document, and it spells out the official attitude of the Seventh-day community towards abortion, and it must be noted that they are not mandatory. Each hospital owned by the SDA denomination is free to develop its own guidelines congruent with the prevailing attitude towards abortion of the community the institution is located in.

The document is readily accessible by Internet, for which reason there is no need to reproduce it here. Here are some of the salient statements describing the SDA community's attitude towards the taking of human life prior to birth:

> *"Many contemporary societies have faced conflict over the morality of abortion. Such conflict also has affected large numbers within Christianity who want to accept responsibility for the protection of prenatal human life while also preserving the personal liberty of women.*

---

[135] Seventh-day Adventist Church. Adventist Beliefs/Guidelines: *Guidelines on Abortion* (12 October 1992). www.adventist.org/beliefs/guidelines/main-guide1.html

> *"The need for guidelines has become evident, as the Church attempts to follow scripture, and to provide moral guidance while respecting individual conscience. Seventh-day Adventists want to relate to the question of abortion in ways that reveal faith in God as the Creator and sustainer of all life and in ways that reflect Christian responsibilities and freedom."*

Notice the emphasis on *"liberty,"* *"individual conscience,"* and *"freedom,"* which are the strongholds of the defenders of abortion, and bear in mind that right at the beginning of this document there is a clear reference to the *"protection of prenatal human life,"* which sounds very much like a pro-life statement. Nevertheless, this seemingly pro-life declaration is neutralized by references to *"personal liberty of women,"* *"individual conscience,"* and *"freedom"!* Does this statement agree with what the pioneers said about abortion? Did the early leaders of the SDA church ever make any reference to *"personal liberty of women,"* *"individual conscience,"* or *"freedom"?* The answer is "No." What else of significance is there in these guidelines?

> *"Prenatal human life is a magnificent gift of God. God's ideal for human beings affirms the sanctity of human life, in God's image, and requires respect for prenatal life. However, decisions about life must be made in the context of a fallen world. Abortion is never an action of little moral consequence. Thus prenatal life must not be thoughtlessly destroyed. Abortion should be performed only for the most serious reasons."*

 Notice that this statement placed the church in the pro-choice camp. How can the killing of an innocent human life be equated with *"respect for prenatal life"?* As we continue reading the document, we will discover that the *"serious reasons"* justifying abortion include even the mental health of the pregnant woman, which is what opened the door for elective abortions in our hospitals.

There are references to the *"sanctity of human life,"* and *"respect for prenatal life."* But these pro-life declarations are again tempered and modified by a suggestion that *"decisions about life must be made in the context of a fallen world,"* that *"abortion should be performed only for the most serious reasons,"* and that *"attitudes of condemnation are inappropriate in those who have accepted the gospel."*

In light of the strong and unambiguous condemnation of the practice of abortion by the early pioneers of the Seventh-day Adventists Church--with no exceptions--can the current SDA official position on abortion be equated with that of the early SDA Church?[136] The answer is "No." of course!

> *"Abortion is one of the tragic dilemmas of human fallenness. The Church should offer gracious support to those who personally face the decision concerning an abortion. Attitudes of condemnation are inappropriate in those who have accepted the gospel. Christians are commissioned to become a loving, caring community of faith that assists those in crisis as alternatives are considered."*

Imagine for a moment that instead of abortion we were discussing other less  harmful actions such as theft, rape, or the sexual abuse of children. Would it be appropriate to argue that *"attitudes of condemnation are inappropriate in those who have accepted the gospel"*? It is true that Jesus said to the adulterous woman *"Neither do I condemn thee,"* but Jesus did not approve the woman's sinful behavior, because he added: *"Go and sin no more."* This is a clear indication that Jesus did not approve the woman's former lifestyle. This is where we as a church have failed. Jesus did not condemn the woman who was caught in a sinful act, but he did disapprove her former lifestyle.

Can we define the current SDA position on abortion as pro-life, given the clear opposition to abortion by the early leaders of the SDA Church? The contrast between the current SDA attitudes towards abortion and that of the SDA pioneers seems to be very clear. In addition, it might be reasonable to

---

[136] See my description of the SDA early pioneers' attitude towards abortion.

wonder whether the current soft attitude towards the taking of human life during pregnancy would encourage our preachers and writers to imitate the strong and determined opposition towards the practice of abortion exhibited by the original founders of the SDA movement. But, there is more in said document:

> *"The Church does not serve as conscience for individuals; however, it should provide moral guidance. Abortions for reasons of birth control, gender selection, or convenience are not condoned by the church. Women, at times however, may face exceptional circumstances that present serious moral or medical dilemmas, such as significant threats to the pregnant woman's life, serious jeopardy to her health, severe congenital defects carefully diagnosed in the fetus, and pregnancy resulting from rape or incest. The final decision whether to terminate the pregnancy or not should be made by the pregnant woman after appropriate consultation."*

What kind of guidance did our church provide to women facing abortion?  Was profiting from elective abortions the kind of guidance those women needed? Was that the best way to show *"respect for prenatal life"*? If the church saw no wrong from financially benefiting from the killing of innocent children, can we expect Adventist girls and woman to see the evil of sacrificing their own flesh and blood on the altar of convenience and lifestyle? What benefit do unborn children derive from the fact that we describe *"prenatal human life"* as *"a magnificent gift of God"* if we cut their life short before they have had a chance to take their first breath and profit from it?

 These official declarations need to be compared with those of James White, John Harvey Kellogg, J.N. Andrews and others. Do we notice a shift in our SDA attitudes towards abortion as we compare them? Can the reader visualize any of those pioneers suggesting that a woman's *"health"* might be an appropriate justification for the killing of the unborn? Would the early leaders of the SDA Church have considered a woman's health of more import than the life of the unborn?

Would they morally equate the value of human life with human health? Given the many instances when the health of the pregnant woman is affected by her pregnancy, would those pioneers have allowed such an exception to their strong opposition to abortion? If they had considered such an exception, would their strong condemnation of the practice of abortion have made any sense? Now look at the following statement found in the same church document:

> *"Christians acknowledge as first and foremost their accountability to God. They seek balance between the exercise of individual liberty and their accountability to the faith community and the larger society and its laws. They make their choices according to scripture and the laws of God rather than the norms of society. Therefore, any attempt to coerce women either to remain pregnant or to terminate pregnancy should be rejected as infringements of personal freedom."*

 How can we argue that we make our *"choices according to scripture and the laws of God rather than the norms of society"* if we are by our own behavior violating God prohibition against murder? By justifying abortion and by profiting from it we are giving undeniable evidence that in fact we are following the *"norms of society"* instead of *"the laws of God."* This fact is so clear that even a blind man can see the deception contained in those declarations. The prevailing liberal norms of society have been substituted for the laws of God. The shedding of innocent blood is condemned throughout Scripture and a violation of God's Holy Law.

We need to compare these statements with those of the early pioneers of the SDA Church. Had James White, John Harvey Kellogg, or J.N. Andrews been subject to similar *Guidelines on Abortion*, would they have been able to speak so clearly against the practice of abortion?

Would they have issued such strong condemnation against the taking of human life? No wonder our modern SDA preachers avoid the subject in their sermons. If they were to imitate those SDA pioneers, they would be in violation of our *Guidelines on Abortion*.

 A few years ago a retired SDA treasurer asked his Loma Linda University Church SDA pastor why he never preached about abortion. To which the pastor replied: *"I couldn't do that. Some of the members of my church might be offended."* Can we picture men like John the Baptist, or the prophet Elijah, giving such an answer? Notice also this comment:

"God gives humanity the freedom of choice, even if it leads to abuse and tragic consequences. His unwillingness to coerce human obedience necessitated the sacrifice of His Son."

This statement located towards the end of the document is quite telling. It suggests that Jesus died in order that women might have the freedom to kill

 their unborn children. If this is the case, then someone might add that Jesus perhaps also died that we might be free to rape, steal, and murder! Does this make any moral sense? James White and the founders of the Adventist movement would probably respond that Jesus died to free us from our sins

instead of granting us the freedom to sin. People are free to shoot at the president, but there are serious consequences for such an action. They may end in jail or the electric chair.

Considering the striking contrast between the attitudes towards the practice of abortion by the founders of Adventism when compared with the current SDA attitudes as revealed by the SDA official document on abortion, the reader would probably agree that there is no other logical alternative but to conclude that, if the *Guidelines on Abortion* truly reflect the thinking of the SDA community, then these statements seem to suggest that modern SDAs are rather pro-abortion instead of pro-life.

 I did use the pro-abortion category here because there is very little difference between the pro-choice and pro-abortion alternatives. They are the same enchilada with a

slightly different ingredients. Both positions lead to elective abortions. or abortions on demand. It is true that the guidelines include many pro-life references such as the following:

- *"Prenatal human life is a magnificent gift of God. God's ideal for human beings affirms the sanctity of human life, in God's image, and requires respect for prenatal life."*
- *"Abortion should be performed only for the most serious reasons."*
- *"Abortion is one of the tragic dilemmas of human fallenness."*
- *"abortions for reasons of birth control, gender selection, or convenience are not condoned by the church."*
- *"Human life has unique value because human beings, though fallen, are created in the image of God."*
- *"God values human life not on the basis of human accomplishments or contributions but because we are God's creation and the object of His redeeming love."*
- *"God calls for the protection of human life and holds humanity accountable for its destruction."* And
- *"God is especially concerned for the protection of the weak, the defenseless, and the oppressed."*

Nevertheless, the force of these pro-life statements is neutralized by many other statements that clearly emphasize personal freedom, individual conscience, exceptional circumstances, and freedom of choice; which requires the placement of the modern SDA denomination in the pro-choice/pro-abortion camp as evidenced by the above referenced official document.

Notice that said document states that elective abortions are *"not condoned by the church."* How can we make such a declaration if we have been offering abortions on demand since 1970? Who are we trying to deceive? This kind of apparent contradiction is reminiscent of what Pilate did: He ruled that Jesus was innocent of any crime but condemned him to death. Likewise, we did declare in our guidelines that we do not condone elective abortions but we did allow our own medical institutions to profit from them. The non-

Adventist world can easily see the contradiction between what we preach and what we do, and our actions speak louder than our words!

I must note that neither the Catholic Church nor the Southern Baptist Convention have any guidelines on abortion, because they opted for a pro-life position: No abortion. Period! The *Guidelines on abortion* were created precisely because the SDA church adopted a pro-choice/pro-abortion position on abortion. If the SDA church were pro-life, there would be no need for guidelines on abortion. Said guidelines became necessary in order to provide a justification for our mistaken belief that we can please both God and the world at the same time. This document was created to redefine God's dictum against murder.

The reader might be aware that the majority of Seventh-day Adventists, with the exception perhaps of those working in the medical field, have probably never read the *Guidelines on Abortion*, and may not even be informed of the existence of such a document, which shows the need to study this relevant topic with a humble attitude of prayer asking God to revive the true faith given to the saints.

Why Silence is not an Option
by Lincoln E. Steed

Lincoln E. Steed, Editor of *Liberty Magazine*, a Seventh-day Adventist publication whose objective is to advance the protection of religious liberty, wrote an editorial in 2004 entitled *"Why Silence is not an Option."*[137]

It deals with the Seventh-day position on gay marriage and the alleged homosexual rights, but what he stated is true as well about the wanton destruction of human life prior to birth.

---

[137] Lincoln E. Steed, "Why Silence is not an Option" *Liberty Online* (Sept./Oct. 2004). http://www.libertymagazine.org/article/why-silence-is-not-an-option

There is a biblical principle that states that failure to speak up when the opportunity arrives means tacit approval. Let's take a look at what Steed wrote:

> *"In discussions with a particular pastoral candidate local church elders informed him that should he come to their church, he was not to mention a word about same-sex relationships. No sermons, no Bible studies, no church discipline, could be administered over the issue. Silence on the matter was not only expected; it was demanded of the pastor. In good conscience the pastor decided that that church was not for him. He went elsewhere to minister. One could perhaps understand if the church that made such a demand were of a liberal mainline denomination. However, such was not the case. It was a local church in my own denomination–Seventh-day Adventist."*

Using this incident as an illustration, Steed makes a case for eliminating  silence as an acceptable moral option when dealing with moral.principles If the church cannot afford to be silent on the issue of same-sex marriage, which deprives nobody of life, then how can Seventh-day Adventists opt to be neutral--pro-choice--or silent in the much more serious matter of abortion which has deprived over 56 million unborn babies of life?

REDEFINING PERSONHOOD

 Another book written by a Seventh-day Adventist author is *What Is a Person? An Ethical Exploration,*[138] published in 1997. It reflects the thinking of a highly respected Loma Linda University faculty member, James W. Walters. His expertise is rooted in the realms of theology, philosophy, and ethics. On the front inside cover flap, we find an explanation for the writing of this book:

> *"When does a person qualify for protected and continuing life? At a time when technology can sustain marginal life, it is ever more important to understand what constitutes a person. What are the medical, ethical, mental, legal, and philosophical criteria that determine protectable human life?"*

 If the previous publication of another book in 1992, *"Abortion: Ethical Issues and Options,"* edited by David Larson, and the adoption of the official *Guidelines on Abortion* in the same year can be considered as having dealt a fatal blow to the growing pro-life movement within Seventh-day Adventism, then the publication of James W. Walters book might represent the last nail in the SDA pro-life coffin.

A Brief Review of Walter's Book

Walters started his book with the following question: *"Are persons and humans equivalent terms? Are all persons humans? And are all humans*

---

[138] James W. Walters. *What Is a Person? An Ethical Exploration* (Urbana and Chicago, Illinois: University of Illinois Press, 1997), 1-181. At the time of the publication of this book, Walters held the position of professor of ethical studies at Loma Linda University, and editor of Who's to Live: Ethics and Aging and Facing Limits: Ethics and Health Care for the Elderly. The illustrations were supplied by the author of this dissertation.

persons?"[139] Why did Walters ask these questions? The answer lies in the fact that he doesn't believe that a conceptus, the size of a pencil dot, can be equated with that of a fully developed individual *"who possesses a degree of self-consciousness."[140]* He is convinced that self-consciousness is an indispensable requirement for personhood.[141]

 To these two examples Walters added the cases of anencephalic infants who are forever beyond any hope of developing neo-cortical functions. Modern medical technology provides the means for sustaining human life under those conditions almost indefinitely. Of course, medical care for these special cases doesn't come cheap, for which reason society can't avoid the question: *"How do we decide who has a special moral claim to life and scarce medical resources?"* Walters' answer is:

> *"The more nearly an individual human or animal approximates a life of self-consciousness, the greater the claim of that individual to maximal moral status."*

Of course, Walters fails to specify how long society should wait before a patient is determined to be *"irretrievable beyond consciousness."* There have been documented cases where patients have regained consciousness after years of being in a comatose state.

Needless to say, this represents a radical departure from the position held by the early pioneers of the SDA church and from the value assigned by God to human beings. Aren't we told that God would have died even for one human being? Does this exclude the unborn or the less than perfect baby waiting for the chance to take its first breath?[142] Then he added the following:

---

[139] Ibid., 1.
[140] Ibid.
[141] Ibic.,3.
[142] Ibid., 5.

110

> *"The proximate personhood model contends that the greater the potentiality for and the greater development toward uncontested personhood and the greater the binding of persons to the baby, the greater the newborn's moral standing."*

This last statement would be considered anathema to pro-life individuals who view human beings as possessing intrinsic moral value regardless of their intelligence, self-awareness, size, location, or pragmatic contribution to society. They believe that only God possesses the ability to assess the correct moral value of human beings.

 Walters concluded his introductory chapter by explaining his special interest in elucidating the case of anencephalic infants: They can be valuable sources for organs donations that could benefit patients who are dying for a lack and scarcity of such organ donors. Walters stated he would like to have the law altered so that this source of human organs might become available to medical experts.

If anencephalic infants possess less moral value than normal human beings, then Walter's argument makes sense; nevertheless, if human beings have intrinsic moral value regardless of their mental condition, then it would be immoral to sacrifice their lives in order to save the life of others. Much less remove their vital organs while they are still breathing, which is what science wants in order to secure fresh human organs for transplantation purposes.

 My view is that this humanistic approach to human moral value contrasts greatly with the one exhibited by Jesus Christ. Those who brought the adulterous woman to Jesus considered that she had no right to life, and they were ready to stone her. Jesus thought otherwise. When children tried to get close to Jesus, his disciples believed that they were not entitled to such a privilege. Jesus said: *"Let the children come to me!"*

In God's eyes, those with greatest needs possess the greatest moral value. This means that the children, the unborn, the newborn, the handicapped, the disabled, and the comatose, might possess a higher moral value than those who have no special needs. Jesus portrayed himself as the good shepherd who left the 99 sheep who were safe in the fold, and went in search of the one that got lost.

No doubt, the recipient of the transplant organ might have a better chance of enjoying life than the anencephalic or comatose patient, but does quality of life justify taking the life of someone who is not dying? Walters attempted to buttress his argument by reminding us what happened in 1986; but he forgot that two wrongs do not make either one of them right.[143]

> *"Currently, most organs come from infants who suffer traumatic deliveries, are victims of child abuse, or are involved in automobile accidents. . . . Theoretically, a single anencephalic infant with healthy thoracic and abdominal organs could supply vital organs to save the lives of two other children (one needing a heart and another a liver)."*

Walters added that most anencephalic newborns are either dead at birth or else die within days of birth, but this argument would fail to convince pro-lifers. How can the prognosis of the shortness of a human life justify the murder of a patient?

For the success of tansplantation, the human organ must be removed from a person that is breathing, otherwise the organ is useless. When a person is dead, his organs are dead as well! Does redefining the death criteria solve the moral problem?

 Following the successful transplantation of a heart from anencephalic Baby Gabrielle to baby Paul Holc at the Loma Linda University Medical Center, a debate ensued about the ethical implications of the use of organs from anencephalic children. The Canadian Pediatric Society issued a ruling in 1990 stating that in the case of anencephalic children, a whole brain death was a prerequisite for the use of organs from said children.

---

[143] Ibid., 113-114.

The problem is that *"testing for brain death in newborns is not as reliable as is for older children."*[144] One solution proposed is to alter the law from whole-brain death to cerebral-brain death. Of course, the American public is *"not ready or willing to equate anencephaly with death."*[145] Walters seemed inclined to such an alteration of public policy, and he is not alone in this endeavor:[146]

> *"A significant number of leading physicians and bioethicists are philosophically open to a change in current law that would allow organ procurement from anencephalic infants immediately after birth."*

Perhaps the public is not ready because altering the criteria for determining death will not change the fact that these anencephalic children are alive. Removing vital organs from a live human being is morally abhorrent, especially for those affiliated with the pro-life movement.

In his last chapter, *"Anencephalic Infants and the Law,"*[147] Walters documented the exceptional case of Baby K, whose mother refused to have an abortion when her physician informed her that her unborn baby was an anencephalic case. After birth, the newborn was placed on a ventilator, and her pediatrician asked her to authorize the removal of the ventilator. She again refused. The hospital went to court in order to force the removal of the ventilator. The judge sided with the mother and the newborn baby remained alive for two years and a half.

If Walter's proposal were to be implemented, a death certificate for Baby K would have been issued two years prior to the time he stopped breathing. When a physician declares a baby dead, you bury the infant. Would society condone burying a baby that is still breathing?

In another case, the Florida court ruled that the parents of an anencephalic baby could not donate the baby's organs until the newborn was dead. The baby's parents appealed to the state Supreme Court without success.[148]

---

[144] Ibid., 122.
[145] Ibid., 129.
[146] Ibid., 139.
[147] Ibid., 140.
[148] Ibid., 141.

> *"I can't authorize, someone to take your baby's life, however short, however unsatisfactory, to save another child. Death is a fact, not an opinion."*

 The problem with anencephalic babies is that they do not have a *"higher"* brain, although their brain stem is intact. Prompted by this medical fact, in 1986 California State Senator Milton Marks introduced a bill that would have defined anencephalic babies at birth as dead. Loma Linda University Professor Gerald Winslow declared that such a change in the definition of death was absurd in spite of the fact that anencephalic babies are never likely to experience consciousness.

Pro-lifers might ask: How can science declare the higher brain of an anencephalic baby dead if, according to their own admission, the newborn doesn't have a higher brain to begin with? How can they say that an anencephalic newborn is dead, and then instruct the hospital caretakers to maintain the baby alive until the organ can be harvested? If the babies were really dead, there would be no need to maintain them alive until the organs are harvested!

 Can someone remove a beating heart from a baby without killing the infant? And how can a physician issue a death certificate for a newborn anencephalic if the baby's heart is still beating? These are hard questions for those who would like to redefine death. Reacting to these efforts to redefine death, the President's Commission developed the Uniform Determination of Death Act, which requires the following:[149]

> *"(1) cessation of respiratory functions, and (2) irreversible cessation of all brain functions, including those of the brain stem."*

---

[149] Walters, 148.

Nevertheless, the American Medical Association judicial council determined in 1986 that the removal of treatment and intravenous nutrition from a permanently comatose patient was permissible.

Walters suggested that *"it is time to realize that when there is no personal life, the individual is dead,"*[150] that parents should be allowed to choose their preferred definition of death from the following options: (1) cardio-respiratory death, (2) whole-brain death, or (3) higher-brain death. And he offered the following reason for his proposal:[151]

> *"Parents already make vital decisions about their offspring when they consider abortion—within legal limits. If making such decision in regard to healthy fetuses is permissible, it should be permissible for parents of higher-brain-absent newborns to consider their tragic infants to be legally dead."*

Pro-lifers would counter that a bad decision cannot be validated on the basis on a worse one. They might agree that killing an anencephalic baby makes more ethical sense than taking the life of a healthy fetus, but the problem is that both actions are morally wrong. Besides, there is a higher redeeming value in saving someone else's life than preserving the lifestyle of the pregnant woman.

Final Observations and Remarks

In this chapter the writings of only one individual were considered, James W. Walters, the author of the book *What is a person?* and his position on abortion is pro-choice. He is also among the first leading Adventists to publicly admit this fact! Following the publication of this book, Dr. Dalton Baldwin's Schumann Pavilion Sabbath School Class in Loma Linda devoted one Sabbath to the study of each chapter contained therein. On one of those Sabbaths, Dr. Fritz Guy, a respected La Sierra University professor, led the discussion, and he made the following observation about the alleged purpose

---

[150] Ibid., 149.
[151] Ibid., 151.

of Walter's book: To facilitate the procurement of human specimens for scientific research.

Of course, if science is allowed to redefine the meaning of death, then live human organs can be harvested from live [now labeled as dead] human beings. The objective is laudable: saving human lives. The moral question is: Is it ethically acceptable to cut short the life of one human being in order to prolong the life of another, and without that individual's consent? Would a loving parent allow the harvesting of an organ from a dying son or a daughter in order to prolong his own life? Shouldn't society allow the Golden Rule to prevail when dealing with organ transplantation?

Note: For my full review of James Walters book *"What is a Person?"* see Chapter X of my book *"From Pro-life to Pro-choice: The Dramatic Shift in Saeventh-day Adventists Attitude Towards Abortion."*[152] You can order the book from Amazon or from my printer. If you order it from the printer you will save some money.

---

[152]

http://www.lulu.com/shop/search.ep?type=&keyWords=nic+samojluk&sitesearch=lulu.com&q=&x=12&y=12

SHOUTING FROM THE ROOFTOP
Introduction

 Back in the early nineties, my home church published in their church bulletin an open critique of the activities exhibited by pro-lifers. I contacted the editor of the church paper asking for equal time to respond on behalf of those who held the opposite point of view. The editor responded that this would not be possible, since the topic was controversial.

I appealed to the senior pastor of my church, and was told that my response was too long. I then contacted several other SDA official and independent publications hoping that one of those might allow me to defend the pro-life position on abortion. These efforts failed as well. Two of those independent periodicals invited me to submit an article on the topic. I did. That was over a decade ago. I am still waiting for them to publish it.

 This prompted me to try another tactic. I wrote an article entitled *"Beyond Fundamentals"* and submitted it to the *"Adventist Review."* It dealt with a topic that had nothing to do with abortion. The article was accepted for publication, and I received a $50 dollar check in payment for my work. I never saw my literary contribution published.

I then sent a donation to my local church designated for the benefit of pro-life activities. It was returned with the following note: *"The church does not have a pro-life program."* I sent similar donations to the General Conference of SDAs on two separate occasions. They were returned un-cashed with the same explanation.

This frustrating pro-life promotion experience prompted me to start my own Internet web site with an emphasis on news dealing with ethics, morality, religion, origins, and pro-life issues.[153] Since then, I managed to write a large number of articles dealing with religion and ethics. I also succeeded in getting some of my comments on abortion published by some SDA periodicals. Below you will find a small sample of what I published since then; I will devote the rest of my book to said objective. I will start with the following anecdote:

One day I met the wife of a leading member of the Adventist Church at the post office. She asked me how my work on behalf of the unborn was progressing. I shared with her my vision for the Adventist Church and the need for a fundamental reform to our view of the value of human life from the moment of inception regardless of its size, place of residence and stage of development.

 Once I was done with my seemingly eloquent speech, she said: *"You need to shout this message from the rooftop."* I related this incident to my nephew and he remarked: *"Yes, but every time you try to get to the rooftop, someone pulls the ladder from under you."*

This incident explains the collection of articles I am including here which I have written in the last couple of decades and which illustrate my thinking regarding the controversial abortion issue. The publication of my first book and the current one are the result of the fact that every time I attempt to get to the rooftop of the Adventist media, the way to the rooftop is blocked by those in charge of those publications.

I have published all the articles I have written on my own web site[154] and many of them in my first book on abortion.[155] Many others I have written since then. They are not posted in a chronological order here. The first article appearing below was also published by Shane Hilde in his *"Advindicate"* web site, and it generated close to 300 comments from readers.[156] I suggest that you take the time to read the lively exchange of views that took place following the publication of said article.

---

[153] http://sdaforum.com, http://letsfocusonlife.com/, and finally http://adventlife.wordpress.com .

[154] http://adventlife.wordpresss.com

[155] *"From Pro-life to Pro-Choice,"*http://www.lulu.com/shop/search.ep?type=&keyWords=nic+samojluk&sitesearch=lulu.com&q=&x=12&y=12

[156] http://advindicate.com/articles/3008

The Ultimate Form of Child Abuse

Abuse: A Loma Linda University Study

A recently created video by the Loma Linda University [LLU] shows that physical, emotional, and sexual abuse in the Adventist community matches that of society in general. The same is true about the Incidence of abortion.

You can watch the dramatic testimony of several victims of child abuse and how they managed to overcome these dark experiences of their childhood by clicking on the link provided below.[157]

A Study Dealing With the Ultimate Form of Child Abuse?

 As I was watching this video, I wondered if LLU researchers will ever decide to carry out a similar study about the ultimate kind of abuse: abortion. My reasoning is as follows: If child abuse is painful and tragic. What can be as hurtful and damaging as the dismemberment of the body of an unborn child? The victim of child abuse usually survives; the victim of abortion has no such hope. The act is irreversible and final!

Our Adventist Moral Blind Spot

Do I believe that such a study involving the ultimate form of child abuse is likely to take place in the near future at our LLU? I don't think so! My reason is as follows: As a community of faith, we have slowly developed a blind moral spot regarding abortion.

This started approximately half a century ago when the State of Hawaii legalized the practice of killing unwanted unborn children with impunity. This nefarious business proved to be extremely profitable, and our Adventist Church decided to get a share of the pie in spite of the biblical injunction against the killing of innocent human beings.

---

[157] http://adventlife.wordpress.com/2013/01/228/abuse-a-loma-linda-university-study/

The Strong Pro-life Position of Our Adventist Pioneers

Most Adventists are aware that our pioneers were definitely pro-life as evident from the statements made by some of the leaders of the Adventist movement.[158]

 A classic example is a paragraph taken from an article authored by a pro-lifer that James White, the founder of our publishing work, included in his book in which the writer condemned the practice of abortion in the strongest terms:[159]

"Few are aware of the fearful extent to which this nefarious business, this worse than devilish practice, is carried on in all classes of society! Many a woman determines that she will not become a mother, and subjects herself to the vilest treatment, committing the basest crime to carry out her purpose.

And many a man, who has as many children as he can support, instead of restraining his passions, aids in the destruction of the babes he has begotten.

The sin lies at the door of both parents in equal measure; for the father, although he may not always aid in the murder, is always accessory to it, in that he induces, and sometimes even forces upon the mother the condition which he knows will lead to the commission of the crime."

How Did Adventists Manage to Jump Over the Life Fence?

The hard question is: How did a pro-life church manage to jump over the life fence into the pro-choice/pro-abortion camp? A fence so high that even Rome did not dare to scale? And how did we dare to profit from the violation of the Sixth Commandment of the Decalogue written by God's own hand on two tables of stone and the violation of our own Guidelines on Abortion?

---

[158] http://adventlife.wordpress.com/2012/03/02/what-did-our-adventist-pioneers-say-about-abortion
[159] James White, editor. *Solemn Appeal* (Battle Creek, Michigan: Stem Press, 1870), 100.

 n, we need to remember the days when the and the Soviet Union was so hot that the Clock were moved to three minutes before omic Armageddon was augmented by the losion in the country of China, and many world leaders warned that this population explosion was to be feared more than an atomic war.

This obsession with the uncontrolled population growth was complicated by the sudden legalization of abortion in the State of Hawaii where our Castle Memorial Hospital was located. The non-Adventist physicians at said medical facility demanded the right to offer abortion on demand, and our North American Division president, Neal Wilson, caved in to the pressure when he made the following public declaration:[160]

> *"Though we walk the fence, Adventists lean toward abortion rather than against it. Because we realize we are confronted by big problems of hunger and overpopulation, we do not oppose family planning and appropriate endeavors to control population."*

The Inevitable Result of this Change of Policy

Such a drastic change in church policy regarding the sacredness of human life resulted in the participation by many Adventist medical institutions in the profitable business of killing human beings at the most vulnerable season of their lives. Here is a list of medical institutions that participated in this new facet of medical service which involved killing in addition to healing:[161]

---

[160] George Gainer, ""The Wisdom of Solomon"?" Spectrum 19/4 (May 1989): 38-46; "Abortion: History of Adventist Guidelines" Ministry (Aug. 1991): 11-17.
[161] http://www.ministrymagazine.org/archive/1991/August/abortion-history-of-adventist-guidelines

> *"Castle Medical Center, Hadley Memorial Hospital, Hanford Community Hospital, Loma Linda University Medical Center, Porter Memorial Hospital, Port land Adventist Medical Center, Shady Grove Adventist Hospital, Shawnee Mission Medical Center, Sierra Vista Hospital, Walla Walla General Hospital, Washington Adventist Hospital, and White Memorial Medical Center."*

At least five Adventist institutions admitted that their abortion services included elective abortion. This, of course, was done with full knowledge of the leadership of the church and with total impunity,[162] which made Adventist pro-lifers wonder about the apparent double standard applied to abortion:

How can we declare that the Adventist Church does not condone abortions on demand[163] if it allows its own medical institutions to profit from the same? Isn't this what Pilate did when he ruled that Jesus was innocent of any crime, yet he ordered his execution?

The Thrashing of the Hippocratic Oath

 This change in policy regarding the sacredness of human life explains our LLU abandonment of the Hippocratic Oath [HO] that had been in high esteem for two millennia in the West. Many Adventists are not aware of this change. Compare the so called *"Do no harm"* principle contained in the HO with the morally neutral statement included in the LLU *"Physicians Oath."*[164]

The evidence seems to suggest that the abandonment of the HO and its replacement with the Loma Linda University Physicians Oath was done to make room for the offering of abortion services to pregnant women.

---

[162] Gerald R. Winslow, "Abortion Policies in Adventist Hospitals" Specttum 19/4 (May 1989): 47-50.
[163] http://www.adventist.org/beliefs/guidelines/main-guide1.html
[164] http://www.nlm.nih.gov/hmd/greek/greek_oath.html;
http://www.susqneuro.com/publications/oaths/index.html#The

> *"I will not give a lethal drug to anyone if I am asked, nor will I advise such a plan; and similarly I will not give a woman a pessary to cause an abortion. I will maintain the utmost respect for human life. I will not use my medical knowledge contrary to the laws of humanity. I will respect the rights and decision of my patients."*

> *"I will maintain the utmost respect for human life. I will not use my medical knowledge contrary to the laws of humanity. I will respect the rights and decision of my patients."*

Notice that the abortion prohibition was replaced by the *"will respect the rights and decision of my patients."* The obvious purpose of this drastic change was to allow for the provision of abortion services in our LLU medical facility.

Seemingly no one has recorded a formal protest against such a fundamental alteration of our traditional respect for human life, except for one LLU professors: Ingrid Blomquist, MD, an associate professor in the school of medicine:[165]

Conclusion

Considering all of the above, my conclusion is that there is an urgent need to restudy our policy of abortion and a need to pay attention to the ultimate form of child abuse: abortion. Yes, there is money to be made out of the killing of innocent human beings who are eagerly waiting to see the light of day.

I am not calling for a window dressing—this has already been done with great success! I am calling for a radical treatment for this moral cancer that is threatening the vitality of our God-given mission to the world. I am calling for the thrashing of *our "Guidelines on Abortion,"* and the restoring of the

---

[165] http://www.llu.edu/pages/faculty/directory/faculty.html?uid=IBlomquist

Hippocratic Oath.

There is no need for any guidelines that negate the crystal clear prohibition contained in the Sixth Commandment of the Decalogue. God's unambiguous directive needs no redefinition! We need to restore all Ten of God's Rules for human behavior to the place of honor they originally had when the Adventist movement was born!

Has Loma Linda University altered the Hippocratic Oath?

 A few years ago, Wesley J. Smith, wrote an article entitled *"Loma Linda University Also Has Weakened the Hippocratic Oath."* Is this true? A simple answer is *"Yes,"* but so have done many organizations in the past. The main question is not whether the Oath has been updated, but rather what has been altered to make room for the wanton killing of innocent unborn victims.

> *"Over the centuries, it has been rewritten often in order to suit the values of different cultures influenced by Greek medicine. Contrary to popular belief, the Hippocratic Oath is not required by most modern medical schools, although some have adopted <u>modern versions</u> that suit many in the profession in the 21ˢᵗ century. It also does not explicitly contain the phrase, "First, do no harm," which is commonly attributed to it. ..."*

Nevertheless, the *"do no harm"* can be deduced from statements like this one contained in the original version of the Hippocratic Oath:[166]

> *"I will not give a lethal drug to anyone if I am asked, nor will I advise such a plan; and similarly I will not give a woman a pessary to cause an abortion."*

---

[166] http://www.nlm.nih.gov/hmd/greek/greek_oath.html

The Loma Linda University Physician's Oath

Now, let's compare this *"do no harm"* feature contained in the original Hippocratic Oath with the following statement contained in the Loma Linda University *"Physician's Oath:"*[167]

> *"I will maintain the utmost respect for human life. I will not use my medical knowledge contrary to the laws of humanity. I will respect the rights and decision of my patients."*

Notice that the *"I will not give a lethal drug to anyone if I am asked, nor will I advise such a plan; and similarly I will not give a woman a pessary to cause an abortion"* has been replaced with the enigmatic statement quoted above which contains an internal logical contradiction:

What happens when the decision of the patient is to end his/her life or request medication or treatment designed to end the life of the unborn baby a woman carries inside her womb? How can a physician comply with his promise *to "maintain the utmost respect for human life"* under those circumstances? Can the physician comply with the requirements of the Physician's oath and the wishes of the patient at the same time?

It is evident that sometimes the *"I will respect the rights and decision of my patients."* is antagonistic to the *"do no harm"* deduced from the original Hippocratic Oath. Anybody who has ever carefully examined the Adventist *"Guidelines on Abortion"* document has probably discovered the same contradiction in said document.

Said guidelines state that human life is a magnificent gift from God which needs to be protected, but the same document enumerates a long list of circumstances under which said protection can be removed from the unborn, including when the woman is depressed and appeals to the mental health exception, thus rendering the protection of the unborn baby null and void.

---

[167] http://www.susqneuro.com/publications/oaths/index.html#

Of course, this undeniable desire to ride the fence of the abortion divide can be easily explained if we discover that both documents originated in our Loma Linda University which had a vested interest in abortion and human organ transplantation. Such a task should have been assigned to an unbiased entity instead. The Adventist leadership simply placed their stamp of approval on what was created in their flagship educational institution.

 This explains also the contradiction found between the church's assertion that the church does not condone abortions on demand, when the evidence is undeniable that the church has allowed some of their hospitals to offer elective abortions with impunity starting as far back as 1970—three years before the abortion option was legalized in the U.S. mainland.

In spite of the above, I want to recognize that there is in our Loma Linda University a physician who still adheres to the Hippocratic Oath in spite of the watered down version adopted by this renowned medical institution owned and operated by the Adventist Church:

Ingrid Blomquist, MD
Associate Professor, Medicine
School of Medicine

> *"Dr. Blomquist is Board certified in Internal Medicine and Infectious Diseases. She has been elected a Fellow of the American College of Physicians and a member of the Alpha Omega Alpha Honor Medical Society. Being a Hippocratic Physician, she has taken, and continues to believe in the principles of the Hippocratic Oath. ..."*

Someone may ask: Does Ingrid Blomquist adhere to the original Hippocratic Oath over two millenia ago? Of course not. The most recent version of said oath which still contained the prohibition against abortion is the one known as the Geneva Oath:

The Hippocratic Oath (Geneva, 1948)[168]

> *"I will maintain the utmost respect for human life, from the time of conception, even under threat I will not use my medical knowledge contrary to the laws of humanity. I make these promises solemnly, freely, and upon my honor. ..."*

Can a Church be Neutral on Moral Issues?

Recent events in the African country of Kenya forced our Adventist Church to make a moral decision, and our leadership decided to declare its neutrality on the issue of abortion, which is definitely a moral issue. So my question is: Can a church be neutral on morality? If a church decides to be neutral on morality, then what is its role in society? Is it to say: "We are neutral on sin, perversion, rape, sexual abuse of children and murder?

Was this the attitude of the prophets in the Old Testament? Did they say: "There are two sides in this moral issue, and we have chosen to remain neutral? Was John the Baptist neutral on moral issues? Why was his head chopped off? And why was Jesus crucified? Was this because he was neutral on justice and truth? Were the disciples of Jesus also neutral on morality?

What Happened in the Country of Kenya?

You may wonder: *"What happened in the country of Kenya?"* Under the current law, abortion is illegal in said country unless the life of the pregnant woman is in serious danger, and there is a bill under consideration designed to liberalize such legislation. The protestant majority in the country is opposed to such a change and is actively engaged in defeating the new legislation which would make it easier for women to secure an abortion.

Our Adventist Response to this Political Crisis

---

[168] http://www.llu.edu/pages/faculty/directory/faculty.html?uid=IBlomquist

 So what did our Adventist leaders do in response to this political crisis? Did they join the other protestant organization in its opposition to the liberalization of the existing abortion law which forbids the killing of innocent unborn human beings? Did our church stand firm in defense of the unborn?

Did our leaders side with those who believe in the unborn right to life? Did they decide to speak on behalf of those who cannot speak in their own defense? Did they come in defense of the Sixth Commandment which forbids murder? Not so!

Those leaders declared the church's neutrality on moral issues.[169] If my church can be neutral on murder, why can't we also be neutral on other moral issues like burglary, rape, and the Sabbath?

> *"The church's statement reiterated local Adventist leaders' wishes to remain neutral on the law ...The Adventist world church has never released an official statement on abortion, but it does offer guidelines on the issue."*

Our Adventist Guidelines on Abortion

And what do those guidelines say about abortion? They say the following among other things:[170]

> *"Prenatal human life is a magnificent gift of God. God's ideal for human beings affirms the sanctity of human life, in God's image, and requires respect for prenatal life."*
>
> *"God calls for the protection of human life and holds humanity accountable for its destruction"*

---

[169] http://news.adventist.org/en/archive/articles/2010/05/07/in-kenya-adventist-leadership-distancing-itself-from-proposed-abortion-law
[170] http://www.adventist.org/information/official-statements/guidelines/article/go/0/abortion/6/

> *"God is especially concerned for the protection of the weak, the defenseless, and the oppressed"*
>
> *"Abortions for reasons of birth control, gender selection, or convenience are not condoned by the Church."*
>
> *"Abortion should be performed only for the most serious reasons."*

So far so good! These statements seem to place our church on the side of life. Where is then the church's neutrality expressed by our Kenyan leaders? What are the serious reasons which would justify the killing of the unborn? Keep on reading:

> *"Women, at times however, may face exceptional circumstances that present serious moral or medical dilemmas, such as significant threats to the pregnant woman's life, serious jeopardy to her health, severe congenital defects carefully diagnosed in the fetus, and pregnancy resulting from rape or incest."*

What happened here? The church is saying that if the unborn baby is the result of a sinful act—rape or incest—it is morally acceptable to punish the guilty? No! To punish the innocent! This statement has pushed justice out the window! The church also implies that the handicapped do not deserve to live! They have no right to life! If the unborn has a physical defect or abnormality, it is morally justifiable to kill such individuals before they have taken the first breath.

Now a word of caution: The above statement makes an exception in case where the pregnant woman's life is in serious danger. This does agree with the current Kenyan law. The law does allow abortion when the woman's life is in jeopardy. My view is as follows: The moral duty of a physician is to save human lives; if the doctor can save only one life instead of two, he is still on the side of life.

 But there is another important point here. The above statement makes reference to the health of the woman, and the defenders of abortion have always included the mental health of the pregnant woman as an integral element of the woman's health. This is where the slippery slope is, because all a woman who is faced with an unwanted pregnancy need to do to get rid of her baby is to find a physician who agrees with her that her mental health is being affected by the pregnancy.

The mental health exception is what opened the door for elective abortions that was practiced with impunity in several of our Adventist hospitals. Our Adventist guidelines clearly state that the church does not condone abortions on demand, but what good can this do to the unborn baby if the church is neutral on abortion?

This is why thousands of elective abortions have been performed in some of our Adventist medical institutions.

A woman says: "This pregnancy is affecting my mental health; I cannot sleep nor concentrate on my studies and work. I want an abortion, and bingo! Another innocent baby is executed in order to protect the woman's lifestyle." And here is more:

> *"God gives humanity the freedom of choice, even if it leads to abuse and tragic consequences. His unwillingness to coerce human obedience necessitated the sacrifice of His Son."*

What is the church saying with the above statement? Notice the emphasis on *"freedom of choice."* What does this freedom of choice suggest? It suggests that we do actually have the freedom to murder the unborn with moral impunity.

But this is not all. It also argues that Jesus died in order to grant us the freedom to kill our own children. Well, I always thought that Jesus died to free us from sin—not to protect our freedom to sin!

Conclusion

What can we conclude from all the above considerations? Can we agree with the position of the Adventist Church and its defense of neutrality concerning moral issues affecting out society? You decide! Here is what a highly respected Adventist pioneer said about neutrally on moral and political issues: [171]

> *"You show me a church that fails to take a stand on political issues that involve moral principles, and I'll show you a church that is spineless, irrelevant, and morally bankrupt. . . . No issue is too controversial for us to address and honestly in pages of our church paper."*

---

[171] Uriah Smith. ***Advent Review and Sabbath Herald***. Quoted by P.A. Lorenz. ***Adventist for Life News,*** Vol. III, Issue 3. (n.d., Heritage Edition): 3

FACTS & REFLECTIONS

Seven Facts Showing that Adventists Are Not Pro-life

 On January 29 *"Spectrum Magazine"* published an article entitled *"Ben Carson Joins Newt Gingrich's Anti-Obamacare PAC,"* authored by Jared Wright, and I counted 620 comments on the day of this writing.[172] Why so much interest in the topic? Two reasons: **A**. Dr. Ben Carson is the first Adventist being asked by 250,000 signators so far to run for the 2016 presidential nomination by Republicans, and **B**. At the end of his interview with the Spectrum correspondent, Carson made the following surprising comment:

> *"Abortions that are done on-demand are not within the purview of God's will. We sit around and criticize ancient pagans for sacrificing babies and saying what heathens they were. But are we really any different if we go around killing babies because they're inconvenient?"*

The result so far has been that Carson's supporters are among non-Adventists, while Adventists are his main detractors. One of the bloggers stated that Carson has been roasted by the Spectrum crowd. Another blogger named Billman, challenged me to submit some facts as evidence that the Adventist Church is not pro-life, but rather pro-choice. Here is a copy of my response to him:

****

Billman, I am glad you asked. I will limit myself to a few facts; I can provide more upon request. I do have quite a few, because that was the topic of my doctoral dissertation.

---

[172] http://spectrummagazine.org/blog/2014/01/29/ben-carson-joins-newt-gingrichs-anti-obamacare-pac

Fact One: Our Adventist pioneers were more pro-life than I am. If you need evidence, let me know.

Fact Two: In 1970, when the non-Adventist physicians at our Castle Memorial Hospital [CMH] demanded their right to offer elective abortions on demand, the management panicked and elevated this request to the North American Division [NAD][173]

Fact Three: Neal Wilson, who was the president of the NAD, after consultation, publicly made the following declaration:[174]

> *"Though we walk the fence, Adventists lean toward abortion rather than against it. Because we realize we are confronted by big problems of hunger and overpopulation, we do not oppose family planning and appropriate endeavors to control population."*

Fact Four: The General Conference [GC] delegated the responsibility to draft guidelines on abortion to the newly created Ethics Department at Loma Linda University [LLU]. Of course, LLU had a vested interest in abortion and organ transplantation, the result was a document which contains a lofty statement about the value of human life, but justifies the killing of innocent unborn babies under a variety of circumstances, including when the unwanted pregnancy affects the mental health of a woman. This opened the door wide for elective abortion on demand.

Fact Five: Our Castle Memorial Hospital began offering elective abortions, and soon after other Adventist institutions followed the CMH lead among them Shady Grove Hospital [SGH] and our Washington Adventist Hospital [WAH]. This was documented by the Washington Post more than once and by our own Adventist publications. This prompted a public manifestation with protesters carrying signs which read: *"Thou shalt not kill."*

---

[173] George Gainer: "The Wisdom of Solomon, Spectrum 19/4 (May 1989): 38-46.
" http://www.scribd.com/doc/160731861/The-Wisdom-of-Solomon-or-The-Politics-of-Pragmatism-The-General-Conference-Abortion-Decision-1970-71
[174] Ibid.

Fact Six: A friend of mine called the GC and asked for a confirmation that our church was no longer pro-life but rather pro-choice. She got an affirmative answer with the following surprising comment: *"Our WAH has become an abortion mill."*

Fact Seven: James Walters, a LLU professor, published a book in which he affirmed that our church is now pro-choice regarding abortion—and pro-choice means pro-choice for killing innocent unborn children.

Since I have reached the perfect number—seven—I will stop, but I can provide additional facts upon request. This is the reason our Adventist pastors are afraid to condemn abortion from the pulpit, and the same applies to our media.

The fear of men has replaced the fear of God. God pronounced four words condemning the killing of innocent human beings. We Adventists employed 1314 words to negate what the Lord wrote on tables of stone with his own finger. You can verify this by comparing Exodus 20 with our Adventist *"Guidelines on Abortion."*

We need to repent and thrash our *"Guidelines on Abortion."* Pro-life entities do not need guidelines on murder.

The Long Journey Towards the Eradication of Abortion in Adventism

The dream and prayer of all pro-life Adventists is that God will produce a revival and reformation among his chosen people and that his Holy Spirit will lead the Adventist Church out of the abortion business.

This may sound like a utopic dream, but for the Lord nothing is impossible. What follows is a summary of the main events connected with the Adventist Church involvement with the abortion business and the growing effort by those Adventists who believe in the dignity of human life and who are eager to move towards such a lofty goal.

This report is the result of countless number of hours by a large number of Adventists who love the church and who are also concerned about the suffering of the victims of this modern genocide, including the women affected by it.

1970. Neal Wilson announced that Adventism was leanings towards abortion

Four decades ago the then president of the North American Division made a public declaration that saddened those Adventists that believe in the right to life by all human beings regardless of their stage of development and their place or residence.[175]

> *"Though we walk the fence, Adventists lean toward abortion rather than against it. Because we realize we are confronted by big problems of hunger and overpopulation, we do not oppose family planning and appropriate endeavors to control population."*

1970. Our Castle Memorial Hospital started offering abortions on demand

When the non-Adventist physicians at our Castle Memorial Hospital demanded the right to offer elective abortions to their patients, the fear of God was replaced with the fear of men, morality gave way to profit, and this medical institution was allowed to include killing in its healing program.[176]

1981. Neal Wilson justified the profit from abortion

 This may surprise you, but I have three witnesses who did corroborate the story that Wilson publicly declared that women would go elsewhere for help if we refuse to participate in the abortion business. This way of justifying the killing of unborn babies was mimicked by Dr. Edward Allred, one of the most successful abortionists in California, in an interview conducted at a church meeting.[177]

---

[175] George Gainer, ""The Wisdom of Solomon"?" Spectrum 19/4 (May 1989): 38-46;
[176] Ibid.
[177] http://www.thenarrowwayministries.org/Page/Abortion-The-SDA-Church/154/

1989. Gerald Winslow reported that five Adventist hospitals were offering elective abortions

LLU Gerald Winslow reported that several other Adventist hospitals emulated the lead of Castle Memorial Hospital and started offering abortions on demand.[178]

1989. George Gainer documented the heavy involvement in abortion by our Washington Adventist Hospital [WAH][179]

The Washington Post reported that between 1975 and 1982: our Washington Adventist Hospital had performed 1492 abortions, which is equivalent to 213 per year.

1990. John V. Stevens negated the right to life of the unborn

Perhaps the strongest defense of the practice of abortion by a SDA leader was written by John V. Stevens, Sr., who was occupying the position of Pacific Union Conference Public Affairs/Religious Liberty Director at the time of publication of his article entitled *"Abortion Answers and Attitudes"* by the *Pacific Union Recorder* in 1990.[180]

> *"The best example is Christ who chose to die in order to restore that freedom lost through sin so that all can choose to mold their own destiny. Christ valued choice over life.*
>
> *Every human being, created in the image of God, is endowed with a power akin to the Creator—individuality, power to think and to do. (Education, page 17) This takes place after birth, when the developing baby becomes a person."*

---

[178] Gerald R. Winslow, "Abortion Policies in Adventist Hospitals" Spectrum 19/4 (May 1989): 47-50.

[179] George Gainer, ""The Wisdom of Solomon"?" Spectrum 19/4 (May 1989): 38-46;

[180] John V, Stevens, Sr. "Abortion Answers and Attitudes," Pacific Union Recorder (20 Aug. 1990): 12-13.

1991. George Gainer documented that twelve Adventist hospitals were offering abortion services[181]

Here is the list of Adventist hospitals that were offering abortion services at the time of George Gainer writing.

> *"Castle Medical Center, Hadley Memorial Hospital, Hanford Community Hospital, Loma Linda University Medical Center, Porter Memorial Hospital, Port land Adventist Medical Center, Shady Grove Adventist Hospital, Shawnee Mission Medical Center, Sierra Vista Hospital, Walla Walla General Hospital, Washington Adventist Hospital, and White Memorial Medical Center."*

1991. The Loma Linda University Church "Dialogue" published an editorial critical of pro-lifers[182]

Following the publication of the *"Dialogue's"* editorial critical to pro-lifers, I asked the managing Editor Gina Foster for equal time in defense of the behavior of pro-lifers.

My request was denied, but she did publish the pro-choice/pro-abortion comments of a reader who was in agreement with her views on abortion. This was my first taste of the biased treatment I have received from our Adventist media since then.

1992. The General Conference Autumn Council approved the *"Guidelines on Abortion"*[183]

What God wrote on stone comprised four words: *"You shall not murder."* Those who drafted our *"Guidelines on Abortion"* employed 1314 words in order to justify what the Lord had forbidden.

---

[181] http://www.ministrymagazine.org/archive/1991/August/abortion-history-of-adventist-guidelines
[182] Gina Foster, Loma Linda University Church Dialogue, 09/1991.
[183] http://www.adventist.org/information/official-statements/guidelines/article/go/0/abortion/

1992. A Deafening Silence followed the publication of the *"Guidelines on Abortion"*

Between 1971 and 1996 I counted 95 Readers' comments and articles dealing with abortion in the pages of our *"Ministry"* magazine. The readers'interest in this controversial issue was so great that on July 1988 David Newman wrote the following:

> *"Our articles on abortion have touched a sensitive nerve. We are receiving more email on this subject than on any other recently published article. The letters are running 10 to 1 in favor of the church adopting a stricter standard."*

 Then suddenly, a few years following the publication of our current Adventist *"Guidelines on Abortion"* a long silence ensued on the pages of this periodical. Our official *"Ministry"* magazine, which had been following this controversial debate for many years, suddenly went into a long hibernation and refused to publish anything that dealt with the issue. We suggest you read the special report I wrote about this unusual event entitled *"The Day Ministry Magazine Went Silent on Abortion."* [184]

Many pro-life Adventist leaders left the church; some of them started their own independent ministries; and, believe it or not, some even went as far as joining the Catholic organization due to its strong pro-life position.

1992-1993. Public records documented the number of abortions at our WAH[185]

According to the *"Health Services Cost Review Commission,"* [HSCRC] a State of Maryland agency charged with the responsibility of acting as a

---

[184] http://adventlife.wordpress.com/2012/02/05/hello-world/
[185] http://www.hscrc.state.md.us/

repository of hospital data, the number of abortions performed at our Washington Adventist Hospital for the stated years was:

1992: 547
1993: 287 from January through June [half a year] which gives us an estimated 574/year

1995. I submitted an article to the Adventist Review

The article was approved for publication and I received a $50.00 dollars check for my work. This is now 2014 and I am still waiting for the Review to publish it. This long delay explains my work on behalf of the unborn.

2005. Jan Paulson claimed that the Adventist Church is pro-life[186]

Jan Paulson, the former GC president, publicly claimed that the Adventist Church was pro-life, and this claim was repeated by Allan R. Handysides, the Director of the G.C Health Ministries in a letter he wrote to me in 2009:

"The Seventh-day Adventist Church is extremely 'pro-life." In spite of this claim, Handysides returned my contribution for the pro-life organization of the church explaining that the church did not have such a program.

2006-2010. Public records revealed the drop in the number of abortions at our WAH[187]

I secured the following abortion statistics from the public source named above:

2006: 47
2007: 48
2008:36
2009: 27
2010: 29

---

[186] "Adventists laud Pope for concern on world peace, poverty and family," *Adventist News Dispatch/Southern Asia-Pacific Division of the Seventh-day Adventist Church (11 Mar. 2005).*
[187] http://www.hscrc.state.md.us/

This is explained by the fact that most abortions are now done in abortion clinics.

1996. I Started publishing the SDA Forum[188]

I began publishing the *"SDA Forum,"* which was eventually replaced by *"Let's Focus on Life,'* and more recently by *"Advent Life."* One segment of said online publication deals exclusively with abortion issues as they relate to the Adventist church. The number of items is too large to include in this report.

1998. The Loma Linda University approves the revised Physician's Oath[189]

If you compare the original *Hippocratic Oath*, which forbids abortion, with the *Loma Linda University Oath*, you will discover that said pro-life prohibition is missing and was replaced with a statement which reads:

> *"I will maintain the utmost respect for human life. I will not use my medical knowledge contrary to the laws of humanity. I will respect the right and decision of my patients."*

How can an Adventist physician respect the decision of a woman who has chosen to abort her baby and honor at the same time his respect for human life?

Recently Jack Priest talked to Israel Gama, a representative of our Shady Grove Hospital in Maryland, and asked him several times what did his hospital do when the decision of the pregnant woman is to have an abortion, and his response was that under such circumstances the hospital followed the Adventist Guidelines on Abortion.

Of course, said guidelines were designed to justify the killing of the unborn under a variety of circumstances, including when the unwanted pregnancy interfered with the mental health of the woman.

---

[188] http://adventlife.wordpress.com/abortion-topics/
[189] http://www.susqneuro.com/publications/oaths/index.html

You may be aware that said mental health exception was the opening door for elective abortions or abortions on demand.

The woman says to her abortionist physician: *"I am mentally depressed; I cannot sleep nor concentrate on my work and my studies;"* and bingo! Another innocent baby is sacrificed on the altar of convenience.

2007. Adventist Today published my article dealing with abortion[190]

This action was done at the request of Dr. Erv Taylor. You can read the response of readers in the issues that followed.

2008. I published my doctoral dissertation about Adventism and abortion[191]

The title of the book is *"From Pro-life to Pro Choice: The Dramatic Shift in Seventh-day Adventists' Attitude Towards Abortion"* And it can be ordered from the printer or from Amazon. It is the only Adventist book in print written in defense of the unborn's right to life.

2009. The Adventist Health Care representative admitted the offering of abortion services[192]

A few years ago, when our Adventist Healthcare organization was competing with a Catholic hospital system for the permit to build a new hospital in Maryland, our Adventist representative argued that the permit should be granted to Adventist because we offer abortion as one of the services to the community.

In the event you are one of those who need hard evidence before they will believe that our church is still in the business of profiting from abortion, you need to read what follows.

---

[190] Vol.15, No.1 | Adventist Today "The Puzzling SDA Apathy Towards the Plight of the Unborn" (Jan/Feb 2007). http://www.atoday.org/article/668/magazine/magazine-pdf-archive
[191]
http://www.lulu.com/shop/search.ep?type=&keyWords=nic+samojluk&sitesearch=lulu.com&q=&x=12&y=12
[192] http://ww2.gazette.net/stories/10142009/olnenew222839_32527.shtml

> *"'Adventist Health Care also runs a primary-care clinic for the uninsured in Shady Grove Adventist Hospital's Germantown emergency center. The clinic now has a pre- and post-natal department for uninsured patients that provides family planning,' according to Washington Adventist Hospital's spokeswoman Lydia Parris."*

> *"Adventist HealthCare is owned by the Seventh Day Adventist Church, which has no religious policies governing health care. Adventist hospitals perform abortions and provide a full range of reproductive care"*

2011. Adventists kept up the fight for the right to build the new hospital[193]

Two years later the Adventist argument was still that the competing Catholic organization did not offer full reproductive services to their patients, including abortion.

> *"Reproductive health advocates across the country have raised concerns about religious directives that prevent Catholic hospitals from providing a variety of services, including fertility treatments, abortions, tubal ligations and hormonal contraception."*

2011. The Washington Post reported on the opposition to the Catholic hospital[194]

The following fact was confirmed by the Washington Post the same year:

---

[193] http://www.washingtonpost.com/wp-dyn/content/article/2011/01/06/AR2011010606620.html
[194] http://www.washingtonpost.com/wp-dyn/content/article/2011/01/19/AR2011011905833.html

> *"While acknowledging concerns about religious directives that prevent Catholic hospitals from providing some services, such as fertility treatments, abortions, tubal ligations and hormonal contraception, she concluded that Montgomery County was not an area "that lacks available and accessible options for obtaining these services."*

2011. The Washington Post reported on Adventists and abortion[195]

Here is another report confirming that the issue of abortion was the main point of disagreement between Catholics and Adventists.

> *"Maryland state regulators gave Holy Cross Hospital, a Catholic institution, permission to build a hospital in growing northern Montgomery County, shutting out the Seventh-day Adventists, who also wanted to build a hospital in the area. <u>Some abortion rights advocates</u> opposed Holy Cross's selection because it does not allow abortions."*

> *"The denomination is known for its emphasis on health. Alcohol and tobacco are prohibited and many Adventists are vegetarians. But the denomination may be the only theologically conservative Protestant group that allows elective abortions."*

2011. Ted Wilson admitted that now abortions are performed inside abortion clinics

In 2011, Ted Wilson, the president of the General Conference, did publicly admit in the City of Redlands, California, that most abortions are no longer

---

[195] http://onfaith.washingtonpost.com/onfaith/undergod/2011/01/adventists_and_abortion.html

performed in our hospitals, bur rather inside abortion clinics. Our Shady Grove Hospital in Maryland does have such a clinic, according to newspaper reports. Other hospitals simply rent office space to abortionists. He also stated that the number of abortions in Adventist hospitals are now *"almost down to zero,"* a claim unsupported by public records.

2013. Advindicate reported the naming of a section of a new building in honor of abortionist Edward Allred at our LSU [196]

If you haven't done this yet, I suggest you read the following report entitled *"La Sierra University's Edward C. Allred Center honors notorious abortionist"*

2013. Advindicate published Nic Samojluk's article dealing with abortion[197]

This document lists important events connected with the abortion business.

2013. Religious Liberty.TV published Ben Carson's view on abortion[198]

Published by Michael Peabody, this report includes the following comment:

> *"Dr. Ben Carson, the famous neurosurgeon and subject of the movie* Gifted Hands, *spoke at a Breakfast Benefit for Birth Choice Pregnancy Resource Center in Clarkston, Michigan on Friday, April 12 "where he said the following among many other things: "Think about it. If you are willing to kill an innocent baby, down the line, who else are you willing to kill?"*

2013. Religious Liberty.TV published "The Wisdom of Solomon" by George Gainer[199]

---

[196] http://advindicate.com/articles/2560
[197] http://advindicate.com/articles/3008
[198] http://religiousliberty.tv/dr-ben-carson-asks-pro-lifers-to-speak-up-and-oppose-abortion-mentality.html
[199] http://religiousliberty.tv/the-wisdom-of-solomon-the-seventh-day-adventist-general-conference-abortion-decision-1970-1971.html

This is a scholarly document depicting the history of the Adventist Church involvement with elective abortion that started in Hawaii back in 1970.

2013. Advindicate published another article dealing with abortion[200]

Shane Hilde, the creator of this online publication, published another article with the title: *"Adventists confused about church's position on abortion."* The reader's comment section is still going on and you can add your opinion to it.

2013. La Sierra University reported the naming of a center in honor of notorious abortionist Edward Allred[201]

Our church's involvement with the abortion business is reflected by the following report published by a LSU magazine. Isn't this a tacit endorsement of the abortion genocide that has destroyed fifty-six million innocent lives in our country alone? Of course, this notorious abortionist donated a sizable sum of money to the school.

> *"Welcome to the Edward C. Allred Center for Financial Literacy and Entrepreneurship. This Center, in the La Sierra University School of Business exists to promote free market economics through the education of students, with a focus on Seventh-day Adventist high schools."*

2013. Religious Liberty.TV reported on the honoring of abortionist Edward Allred by LSU[202]

Read the comments posted above.

2013. Retired Businessman Dan Rotthoff mailed 3,000 copies of Randy's Alcorn abortion book

---

[200] http://advindicate.com/articles/2013/12/6/adventists-confused-about-churchs-position-on-abortion
[201] http://lasierra.edu/academics/schools/business/allredcenter/
[202] http://religiousliberty.tv/?s=Edward+Allred

Dan Rotthof did exchange a couple of letters with the General Conference of the Adventist Church. He followed this with the mailing of three thousand copies of one of the best pro-life books ever written to a list of Adventist educators and leaders in the United States.

2013. Baker City Pastor Tony Brandon delivered a sermon about abortion[203]

How many sermons have you heard about abortion by our Adventist pastors? This writer knows only about two of them: Barry Kimbrough and Tony Brandon. Most of our Adventist pastors are afraid to touch this subject. A friend of mine asked his pastor why he never preached about abortion, and he responded with: *"If I were to do this, some of my members might be offended."* Of course, preaching against sin is offensive to the unconverted heart. So what is the duty of a pastor? What does the Bible teach?[204]

New International Version
"Blow the trumpet in Zion; sound the alarm on my holy hill. Let all who live in the land tremble, for the day of the LORD is coming. It is close at hand— "

New International Version
"But if the watchman sees the sword coming and does not blow the trumpet to warn the people and the sword comes and takes someone's life, that person's life will be taken because of their sin, but I will hold the watchman accountable for their blood.'"

2013. Religious Liberty.TV published a transcript of Pastor Tony Brandon's sermon dealing with abortion[205]

---

[203] https://dl.dropboxusercontent.com/u/1192202/SDA_Abortion_0003.wma
[204] Joel 2:1; Eze. 33:6.

You can now not only listen to Pastor Tony Brandon's sermon, but also read the transcript of the same.

Pray for our church, for the unborn, and for the revival of the true Adventist faith!

Reflections on our Adventist Guidelines on Abortion

What follows is a copy of a letter I wrote to a friend of mine who is doing a great work on behalf of the unborn coupled with some reflections of my own regarding the possible significance of the responses we are getting from the General Conference in connection with the issue of abortion.

****

Dear friend,

I noticed that in the recent response you received from the General Conference, you were directed to the Adventist *"Guidelines on Abortion."* Some years ago, I received a similar answer from a representative of the GC, and I found in our Adventist Review magazine the testimony of someone identified as "earlysda" who got the same response.[206]

> *"I have written President Ted Wilson twice about this issue, and both times received a response referring me to the "Guidelines on Abortion" document that the church has. Does our church have "Guidelines on Sabbath-Breaking" or "Guidelines on Stealing" too?"*

****

It looks like the reference to the Adventist *"Guidelimnes on Abortion"* is the standard reponse to everybody who writes to the General Conference

---

[205] http://www.religiousliberty.tv/audio/TonyBrandon-Sermon-Nov2013.mp3
[206] http://www.adventistreview.org/world-news/-u.s.-abortions-hits-lowest-level-since-1973

regarding the issue of abortion. Do we deal that way on other important doctrinal issues? When someone asks us about the Sabbath, for example, do we say: Read our Guidelines on Sabbath Observance? No! We say, Read Exodus 20!

Why is it that when dealing with the violation of the Sixth Commandment instead of the Fourth, we refer people to our humanly created document dealing with abortion instead of the Decalogue? The apparent reason is that we have set aside what God wrote with his own hand on tables of stone and replaced it with rules of our own devising.

Since the creation of the Adventiust movement, we have emphasized the importance of avoiding the substitution of God's Word with humanly devised tradition, and we have blamed Rome for having done that, but we now have made the same mistake. We have replaced God's Word with our own tradition which tends to justify what the Lord has clearly forbidden: the shedding of innocent blood.

 This seems to indicate that we have ceased to be God's chosen people, those who keep God's Commandments, and are no longer God's special people with the last message of hope for a perishing world. My opinion is that it is high time for us to abandon those guidelines on killing the most innocent members of humanity and return to a *"Thus said the Lord,"* because Jesus said: *"Inasmuch as you have done it unto the least of these you have done it to me!"*

If we repent of our departure from the right path, the Lord is merciful and willing to forgive and clean us from all unrighteousness.[207]

New International Version
"When you spread out your hands in prayer, I hide my eyes from you; even when you offer many prayers, I am not listening. Your hands are full of blood!

---

[207] Is. 1:15-18.

Wash and make yourselves clean. Take your evil deeds out of my sight; stop doing wrong. Learn to do right; <u>seek</u> justice. Defend the oppressed. Take up the cause of the fatherless; plead the case of the widow. "Come now, let us settle the matter," says the LORD. "Though your sins are like <u>scarlet</u>, they shall be as white as snow; though they are red as <u>crimson</u>, they shall be like wool."

CONFIRMATION OF OUR MORAL DETOUR

Candid Confirmation of Involvement with the Abortion Business

As I have reported in the past, my personal investigation into the role the Adventist Church has played in the past concerning the abortion business reveals that some of our Adventist hospitals began offering abortions on demand back in 1970—three years prior to the legalization of abortion in the U.S. mainland.

My research revealed solid evidence that thousands of abortions were carried out in some of our Adventist medical institutions—especially Castle Memorial Hospital, Washington Adventist Hospital, and Shady Grove Hospital. The statistics I was able to secure from official public sources show that there has been a drastic reduction in the number of abortion performed in the recent years.

Some Adventists have recently argued that any reference to elective abortions in Adventist medical facilities is old news dating a couple of decades ago. The factual evidence seems to indicate that this is based on wishful thinking. Fresh information coming from our Adventist Health System provides credible evidence that we are not out of the abortion business yet.

Shady Grove
Adventist Hospital

I reported more than once that my communication with the General Conference and our Adventist health institutions came to a stand still following my personal conversation with our president Ted Wilson two years ago. I did write to our Washington Adventist Hospital and our Shady Grove Hospital requesting information regarding abortion. My effort was unsuccessful, but our pro-life friend, Jack Priest, was luckier than I. Here is his report:[208]

150

I will write more later, but I wanted to give you a quick update. I tried to check with Shady Grove itself to ask about abortions and they finally had Ismael Gama call me from Adventist Health Sytems. He was a nice man and there is some good news and some more of the same

They now have procedures in place that suggests they have made a great effort in doing away with as many elective abortions as they can, with counseling steps and so forth. It seems this has greatly reduced the number of abortions done and from what I learned from him, it appears to be true.

However, I kept asking him over and over again if this meant after all the counseling that if the person still wanted the abortion that they would not do it. He kept repeating that they follow the church guidelines on abortion, and as you know those guidelines do not absolutely exclude elective abortions.

I think he is a good and sincere man and does what he can to stop them, but he cannot say they will not do them if requested after all their effort to talk them out of it. I got the sense that was more what he was ordered to tell people than what he wanted to be able to say."

This report is quite revealing, and Jack is right about our Guidelines on Abortion. They not only do not exclude elective abortions but rather make room for them, including the mental health exception which allows a woman to claim that she cannot sleep, nor concentrate on her work or school, and bingo, another innocent baby is sacrificed on the altar of convenience.

Jack's report confirms my previous communication in which I related how, when competing with the Holy Cross Catholic organization for the construction of a new hospital in Maryland, our Adventist Health System representative argued in favor of a permit benefiting the Adventist church

---

[208] Ismael Gama is the *Assoc. Vice President of the Columbia Union Conference of the Seventh-day Adventist Church.*

because we offer abortion services, while Catholics do not do this for moral reasons.

Investigation into our Adventist involvement with the Abortion Industry

Following the publication of my book dealing with abortion and the Adventist Church, I have received many requests for information regarding the number of abortions performed in our Adventist hospitals. I wish I could provide the exact number of such procedures for each Adventist U.S. hospital from 1970—the year our Adventist hospitals were allowed to offer elective abortions to their patients--up to the present. Unfortunately such statistics are not readily available to investigators. I am ready to share some of what I was able to secure from Adventist and non-Adventist sources, plus an estimate of what might be the best guess based on those statistics.

I counted a total of 51[209] Adventist hospitals within the territory of the United Sates, although some of those institutions are comprised of several medical entities. A good example is *Florida Hospital Orlando* composed of seven individual medical institutions; and *Loma Linda University Medical Center* made up of four separate entities.[210] This means that if we include all the Adventist medical establishments which are located in the U.S. the grand total would be more like 60.

What we Know About our Adventist Participation in the Genocide of the Unborn

What do we know about abortion provided by these medical facilities? The answer is that we don't know enough, but what we do know gives us reason for great concern. We do know, for example, that back in 1970, when the State of Hawaii decided to legalize the practice of abortion, the non-Adventist physicians at our *Castle Memorial*

---

[209] http://www.adventisthospitals.info/pages/country_viewphp_1C588F76.html
[210] http://en.wikipedia.org/wiki/List_of_Seventh-day_Adventist_hospitals

Hospital [CMH] requested the right to offer elective abortions to their patients, and the church, after careful deliberations, caved in to those demands.[211]

This action by the leadership of the church made it possible for eleven additional hospitals to offer abortion services to their patients by 1986, and here is the list of these medical institutions:[212]

> *"Castle Medical Center, Hadley Memorial Hospital, Hanford Community Hospital, Loma Linda University Medical Center, Porter Memorial Hospital, Port land Adventist Medical Center, Shady Grove Adventist Hospital, Shawnee Mission Medical Center, Sierra Vista Hospital, Walla Walla General Hospital, Washington Adventist Hospital, and White Memorial Medical Center."*

Abortions on Demand in Several of our Adventist Hospitals

A survey conducted three years later by the Loma Linda University Ethics Department revealed that five of these Adventist hospitals were engaged— like our CMH—in elective abortions.[213] Of course, abortions on demand are in a direct violation of the biblical prohibition against the killing of innocent human beings, and it would be hard to find another group of human beings more deserving of the *"innocent"* label than the unborn; in addition, providing elective abortions also represent a breach of our church *"Guidelines on Abortion"* which do not condone abortions on demand.

A Tragic Moral Detour by the Leadership of our Adventist Church

How can we explain this conundrum? If the church does not approve of elective abortions, how come the church did allow such a contravention of church policy with impunity? The reason is given by the dilemma our CMH

---

[211] George Gainer, ""The Wisdom of Solomon"?" Spectrum 19/4 (May 1989): 38-46; "Abortion: History of Adventist Guidelines" Ministry (Aug. 1991): 11-17.
[212] http://www.ministrymagazine.org/archive/1991/August/abortion-history-of-adventist-guidelines
[213] Gerald R. Winslow, "Abortion Policies in Adventist Hospitals" Specttum 19/4 (May 1989): 47-50.

faced in 1970: Allow the provision of such morally forbidden practice, or else risk financial failure due to loss of revenue. The fear of financial loss replaced the fear of God. The excuse Neal Wilson, the president of the North American Division, gave to the public was as follows:

> *"Though we walk the fence, Adventists lean toward abortion rather than against it. Because we realize we are confronted by big problems of hunger and overpopulation, we do not oppose family planning and appropriate endeavors to control population."*

Imagine the seriousness of an argument as this one: It meant that, since there were too many human beings in the world and that many of them were starving, it was morally acceptable for the *"Remnant"* church of God to start killing some of the most vulnerable members of the human race in the richest country of the world; a country which had an abundant oversupply of food which the U.S. shared with the rest of the world through its food assistance program.

Abortion Statistics for our Washington Adventist Hospital

I wish we would have the abortion statistics for those twelve hospitals listed above. What I have is anecdotic references to what was taking place in some of them, but I don't have the hard facts.

Nevertheless, thanks to the providential connection with a dedicated pro-life blogger who decided to write to me, I was able to locate a significant amount of information related to one of them: our *Washington Adventist Hospital* [WAH] in Maryland.

In addittion, Adventist historian George Gainer, who wrote extensively about this topic in several Adventist publications, provided the following statistics published by the *Washington Post*:[214]

---

[214] http://www.ministrymagazine.org/archive/1991/August/abortion-history-of-adventist-guidelines

154

> *"As to numbers, participants in the "Pastors' Protest Against Abortion" supplied the figure of 1,494 abortions performed at Washington Adventist Hospital from 1975 through July 1982. They said that the medical records office of the hospital supplied these statistics."*

This means that our WAH was averaging 213 abortions per year. Some have suggested that all these abortion might have been of therapeutic kind—resulting from rape, incest, and malformations—but the large number suggests the opposite. Even Planned Parenthood, the main provider of abortions in the world, did acknowledge that this kind of abortions represent a mere two percent of all abortions. Arguing that said abortions were all of the therapeutic kind would mean that had the hospital included elective abortions in their program, WAH would have done 10,650 abortions per year. This means that most likely 98 percent of them were of the elective type.

Abortion Statistics Published by an Independent Investigator

According to an independent investigator named Patrick Murebil, a decade later the same Adventist hospital reported 547 abortions per year;[215] but by

2006 the number of abortions in the same institution dropped to 47, with 48 reported for the 2007 year.[216] Why such a significant drop in the number of abortions; unfortunately both the People at our WAH and the General Conference [GC] are unwilling to assist in this investigation. I did write to the management at WAH and to Dr. Handysides at the GC about three years ago, and I am still waiting for a response. I also wrote to Ted Wilson,

---

[215] http://forums.catholic.com/showthread.php?t=155025&highlight=Seventh+Day+Adventist+Church+Abortion&page=10
[216] http://forums.catholic.com/showthread.php?t=155025&highlight=Seventh+Day+Adventist+Church+Abortion&page=15

the GC president, asking for assistance with my research, but never got an answer.

A Public Source of Abortion Statistics for our Washington Adventist Hospital

This kind of stonewalling by the Adventist leadership prompted me to search for statistics from other sources, which providentially led me to the *Health Services Cost Review Commission,* [HSCRC] a State of Maryland agency charged with the responsibility of acting as a repository of hospital data and the services they provide to the public.[217] From said source I was able to secure statistics for two Adventist hospitals, but I want to focus on one of them for which statistics are available from other sources.

Number of Inpatient Abortions performed at our Washington Adventist Hospital:

    2008: 36
    2009:27
    2010:29

You might be surprised by the apparently sudden reduction in the number of abortions cases in said medical institution. For contrast purposes, let me post here a summary of all the available statistics to me:

Summary of Available Abortion Statistics for our Washington Adventist Hospital

    1975-1982: 1492, which is equivalent to 213 per year
    1992: 547
    1993: 287 from January through June [half a year] which gives us an estimated 574/year

    2006: 47
    2007: 48
    2008:36
    2009: 27

---

[217] http://www.hscrc.state.md.us/

156

So the question is: Why the huge recent drop in the number of abortions performed at the WAH. The answer seems to be quite simple. The older data included both Inpatient and Outpatient statistics, while the newer data is for Inpatient case only. When I contacted the HSCRC requesting the data for the 2008-2010 years, I was informed that the outpatient statistics were not available. This discrepancy in the numbers makes logical sense, since the modern tendency has been to offer abortion services on an outpatient basis.

Does this mean that the number of abortions has decreased? Perhaps, but we cannot be sure about this unless we can secure the missing data for the outpatient cases. Is this feasible?

My personal suspicion is that it is not. If the HSCRC agency cannot provide such data, who can? A correspondent of mine who has close connections with the General Conference office told me that he was informed that the church has made almost impossible for anyone to secure accurate data about abortion statistics in Adventist hospitals. It may take a whistleblower to accomplish this!

I am not giving up on my endeavor to solve this enigma, which has deepened when Ted Wilson, the current president of the GC, publicly announced in 2011 at a public meeting in the city of Redlands that the elective abortions in Adventist hospitals is almost down to zero. The statistics posted above seemed to tell a different story, but I cannot be 100 percent sure until I secure additional statistics My suspicion is that Wilson may be in the dark about what is really taking place inside our medical facilities.

Ted Wilson is determined to push for a revival and reformation in our Adventist Church, and I wish him success. Nevertheless, his success will be very limited unless he decides to include the respect for the right to life of the unborn in his agenda. I have been praying for God's blessings on his work twice a day. It is the first thing I do when I get up in the morning, and the last thing I do before retiring for the night. We need to repent of our participation in the genocide of the unborn! God is patient and merciful, but we need to repent of this great deviation from moral duty. May the Lord bless his church!

Can we Rely on the Elective Abortion Information Coming from the General Conference?

 The recent revelations made by Patricia Moleski, an Adventist whistleblower, regarding the alleged criminal doctoring of hospital records at our Adventist Health System [AHS] forces us to wonder whether we can rely on the accuracy and reliability of the information coming out of the General Conference regarding what is taking place in our hospitals [GC].

If the president of the GC relies on the record kept by the AHS, and if such record is routinely altered by the deletion of adverse events taking place in our Adventist hospitals, then how can we trust on what the GC president says about anything connected with our medical institutions? He can be honest and truthful, but if he is fed false information, then his credibility is damaged.

If an honest man draws water from a well which has been contaminated by someone, his honesty will not miraculously make the water safe for drinking.

In the event you have not heard about Patricia Moleski's claim, let me suggest that you take the time to watch the video she recorded for our benefit in which she relates her experience while working for the AHS until she was fired for refusing to follow orders to delete the true cause of deaths of several patients. Click on the link listed at the bottom of this page and watch the video.[218]

Can we rely on what Ted Wilson said regarding elective abortions?

On February 21, 2011, Ted Wilson, the president of the Adventist Church, publicly declared in the City of Redlands, California, that the church does not condone elective abortions, and that if any such non-therapeutic procedures

---

[218] http://www.youtube.com/watch?v=F91hN9nR1KA

158

are done, they are against church policy; and he added that this kind of abortions are so insignificant that they are *"almost down to zero."*

I was greatly surprised when I heard this assertion. The reason is very simple: I was on the verge of publishing the result of my investigation into the liberal attitude of the Adventist Church towards abortion, and if what Ted Wilson stated was correct, then I needed to verify the accuracy of said information. The statistics I had accumulated up to that point seemed to contradict what Wilson had affirmed.

A request for help ignored by the General Conference

I was willing to postpone the publication of my book if needed so that I could incorporate the latest statistics provided by the church. When the Redlands meeting was over, I asked Wilson for assistance. I requested help with the securing of statistics verifying the fact that elective abortions were in fact *"almost down to zero."* He suggested that I write to Dr. Handysides at the GC. I did, but got no response. I followed this up with another letter plus a letter to Ted Wilson. Almost three years have gone by and I am still waiting for a response.

Given my urgency to publish my book, I searched for other sources for abortion statistics in Adventist hospitals and located a public entity with the help of a pro-life friend. Said data seemed to tell a different story. Looking back, I am glad the people at the GC ignored my request for statistics. Had I received such data from them, I would have ended with false information I could not rely on. Knowing how records at our AHS are allegedly doctored and falsified on a routine basis, I can only thank the GC for stonewalling me.

Documented Facts Related to Elective Abortions in our Adventist Hospitals

There are certain facts which are undeniable since they have been documented by our own experts and which have been published in our periodicals such as our official *"Ministry" magazine, "Spectrum," "Adventist Today,"* and Adventist books in print. In addition, some of said facts have been also published in well known media outlets like the *"Washington Post."*[219]

Fact Number One: We Adventists have led in the legalization of abortion in the United States of America. We started offering elective abortion services to our hospital patients back in 1970—three years before the practice of abortion was legalized in our mainland. If you have any doubt, you can verify this by accessing the sources listed below.

Fact Number Two: The following Adventist hospitals did participate in the offering of abortion services to their patients:[220]

> *"Castle Medical Center, Hadley Memorial Hospital, Hanford Community Hospital, Loma Linda University Medical Center, Porter Memorial Hospital, Port land Adventist Medical Center, Shady Grove Adventist Hospital, Shawnee Mission Medical Center, Sierra Vista Hospital, Walla Walla General Hospital, Washington Adventist Hospital, and White Memorial Medical Center."*

Fact Number Three: At least five Adventist hospitals reported that they were offering elective abortions on demand.[221]

Fact Number Four: The Adventist Church does not condone abortions on demand, but has granted our Adventist hospitals the freedom to do so with impunity. My view is that this is similar to the behavior of Pilate who declared that Jesus was innocent of any crime but granted immunity to those who were determined to have him executed.

---

[219] George Gainer, Letters *Ministry* (May 1988): 27; George Gainer, ""The Wisdom of Solomon"?" Spectrum 19/4 (May 1989): 38-46; George Gainer, "Abortion: History of Adventist Guidelines" Ministry (Aug. 1991): 11-17.

[220] http://www.ministrymagazine.org/archive/1991/August/abortion-history-of-adventist-guidelines

[221] Gerald R. Winslow, *"Abortion Policies in Adventist Hospitals"* Spectrum 19/4 (May 1989): 47-50.

Abortion Statistics from Independent Public Entities

What follows is a summary of statistics showing the number of reported abortions performed in our Washington Adventist Hospital located in the State of Maryland, and let's keep in mind the fact that Adventist operates over fifty hospitals in the U.S. mainland. These statistics were supplied by the following non-Adventist, independent organization: The Maryland *Health Services Cost Review Commission.*

1992: 547
1993: 287 from January through June [half a year] which gives us an estimated 574/year
2006: 47
2007: 48
2008:36
2009: 27
2010: 29
2011: 30

The mysterious sudden drop in the number of reported abortion

How can we explain the enigmatic drop in the number of abortions for the 2006 through 2011 years? What I discovered was that starting with the 2006 year the number of impatient abortion cases were no longer included. Why? I purchased the 2011 copy of the *American Hospital Association Guide* which used to list the names of hospital performing abortions and found out that this information was no longer included either.

Can we conclude that this sudden drop in the number of abortions in our Adventist hospitals has been drastically reduced? Given Patricia Moleski's claim regarding the routine deletion of adverse events from their patient's and employees' records, I conclude that we cannot trust the information contained therein. Their information seemed to have been compromised on a grand scale, which means that we can no longer rely on what we hear being asserted about elective abortions coming from the General Conference.

If you disagree, share with me your reasons for your opinion.

IN SEARCH FOR THE REMNANT CHURCH

 In the last book of the Bible we find a description of God's Remnant people and I was trained to believe from my childhood that said description applies to Adventism because we have been defending the permanence and validity of the Decalogue and the need to keep the Sabbath Holy as a sign of our allegiance to the God who made the heavens, the earth, and the fountain of waters.[222]

King James Bible
"And the dragon was wroth with the woman, and went to make war with the remnant of her seed, which keep the commandments of God, and have the testimony of Jesus Christ."

King James Bible
"Here is the patience of the saints: here are they that keep the commandments of God, and the faith of Jesus."

Does this biblical description of the saints and of God's Remnant people still apply to the Adventist Church today? It did apply to our Adventist church from the time of the early pioneers until 1970 when a fundamental change took place towards one of God's Commandments: the Sixth one that forbids the killing of innocent human beings.

What happened in 1970? The State of Hawaii legalized abortion; the non-Adventist physicians at our *Castle Memorial Hospital* demanded the right to offer abortion services to their patients, and our church caved in to those demands for fear of loosing significant revenue. The fear of men entered

---

[222] Rev. 12:17; Rev. 14:12.

162

through the door, and the fear of God went out the window. This is well documented in Adventist literature.[223]

Then, in 1992, the Autumn Council of the General Conference adopted a 1314-word-document revision of God's Commandment which forbids murder. This document is known as the *"Guidelines on Abortion."* It describes the circumstances under which it is justifiable to ignore what God commanded.

 This, of course, opened the door wide for the offering of abortions on demand which represents not only a violation of the Sixth Commandment but also the violation of our own Guidelines that do not condone elective abortions. This direct and flagrant disregard of what the Lord did prohibit prompted some pro-life Adventists to start searching for the true Remnant church of God.

Of course, such church does not exist at the present time. Because our Adventist church no longer honors all Ten of God's Rules for human behavior. We still pretend to adhere to God's Decalogue, but in practice we only keep Nine of them.

We have deceived ourselves into believing that the Lord will overlook our duplicity because we still worship him on the correct day of the week: the Sabbath. In this, we are repeating the mistake of the Jewish leaders who killed the Son of God and rushed home to keep the Sabbath Holy.

What follows is a collection of articles I have authored that deal with the serious problem we have allowed to develop four decades ago when we compromised with evil for the sake of filthy profit. Some of these articles were included in my first book, while others were written after the publication of *"From Pro-life to Pro-choice,"* which you can order from Amazon or the printer.[224]

---

[223] George Gainer, *The Wisdom of Solomon?* http://religiousliberty.tv/the-wisdom-of-solomon-the-seventh-day-adventist-general-conference-abortion-decision-1970-1971.html

[224]

http://www.lulu.com/shop/search.ep?type=&keyWords=nic+samojluk&sitesearch=lulu.com&q=&x=12&y=12

Sacred Funds: My Personal Dilemma

How should I handle sacred funds such as my tithes and offerings? For six decades my duty was clear: Send them through the official channels of the church. Then I learned that my church was profiting from the killing of the unborn—and I am not talking about the so *called "therapeutic abortions,"* but rather about elective or abortions on demand.

My Moral Dilemma

I asked myself: Should I continue sending my financial contributions to a church that is guilty of violating God's Decalogue and the church own *"Guidelines on Abortion"?* This suddenly became my personal moral dilemma. If I continued my regular financial routine, wouldn't I become an accomplice in the deaths of innocent human beings? A couple of decades ago, I described my moral dilemma through an allegory you can read.[225]

What I learned in Graduate School

Perhaps you are among the many Adventists who still believe that we are truly pro-life. That is what I thought all along, until I decided to perform an investigation, which eventually became the topic of my doctoral dissertation.[226] After several years of research into the Adventist literature, I learned that we are definitely pro-choice on this issue.

Theoretically, we still teach that we do not approve abortions on demand, but we have allowed some of our own hospitals to violate this moral tenet with impunity. In this we have followed the well-known saying: *"Do what I say, but not what I do!"* This is reminiscent of the behavior exhibited by Pilate, who publicly declared that Jesus was innocent, but condemned him to a cruel death.

---

[225] "A Stigmata Case in Loma Linda? http://adventlife.wordpress.com/2012/07/06/a-stigmata-case-in-loma-linda-by-nic-samojluk-4/"
[226] "From Pro-life to Pro Choice,"
http://www.lulu.com/shop/search.ep?type=&keyWords=nic+samojluk&sitesearch=lulu.com&q=&x=12&y=12

A Serious Moral Detour

Maybe you are still unconvinced! If this is your case, let me cite what a former president of the North American Division declared regarding the sudden abandonment of the long-established pro-life leaning of the church defended by the Adventist pioneers:[227]

> *"Though we walk the fence, Adventists lean toward abortion rather than against it. Because we realize we are confronted by big problems of hunger and overpopulation, we do not oppose family planning and appropriate endeavors to control population."*

Can you imagine the president of the NAD of the church arguing that child killing before birth was justified because there was hunger and there were too many people in the world? And do not forget that he said this in the richest country in the world, the one that provided financial remuneration to farmers as a disincentive to the excessive production of food.

This is hard to understand, but the following might help a little. He said this in the midst of the Cold War, when the hands of the symbolic Atomic Clock had been moved to three minutes before Midnight and the fear of the uncontrolled population explosion in the Communist country of China was feared more than an atomic conflagration between the Soviet Union and the United States.

The Corroborated Testimony of Witnesses

I want to add the testimony of a witness of another statement made by the same Adventist leader as he attempted to justify the church's deviation from moral duty. This assertion was corroborated by another Adventist member who confirmed to me the veracity of said public declaration:[228]

---

[227] George Gainer, The Wisdom of Solomon? *Spectrum* 19/4 (May 1989): 38-46.

[228] http://www.thenarrowwayministries.org/Page/Abortion-The-SDA-Church/154/

"We were at Southern Missionary College (called Southern College, today), and it was a Sabbath afternoon, 1981. We were told that the General Conference President - Neal Wilson, was going to be speaking in the afternoon at the College Church, and holding a Question & Answer forum afterwards. We had never heard him speak, so we decided to attend.

After he spoke, someone from the audience raised [his] hand and asked the question, "Why do our Seventh Day Adventist hospitals perform abortions?" Al and I looked at each other in shock and disbelief, we thought, "Surely, OUR church does not perform abortions!" But....Neal Wilson confirmed that the Church hospitals do perform abortions and went on to give the reason why.... He said that if the Church hospitals did not perform abortions, the women would just go to some other hospitals and get them.

We couldn't believe our ears. That was in 1981. It has been 30 years since that time, and our hospitals are still performing abortions. But, as we talk to members of the Church, we are finding out that most members do not know this. The Church has successfully pushed this under the rug, and the members are in the dark."

Pro-life Adventist Leaders Abandon Ship

Am I the only one bothered by this dilemma? The answer is "No." When the controversy over this issue was raging on among Adventists, several rather vocal pro-life leaders among us fought as hard as they could in defense of the unborn's right to life, but the liberal Adventist leaders prevailed, and many of these pro-life leaders left the church; some of them started independent ministries of their own, and some even went back to Rome because of its strong position on the right to life of every human being.

My Realistic Options

What were my options? A. Continue sending my money through the regular channels of the church; B. Send them with a note attached identifying them as pro-life funds; C. Send them to Adventist independent ministries that were sympathetic to the pro-life cause; or D. send them to non-Adventist pro-life organizations.

I eliminated the first option because it would create a guilty conscience for me. I tried the second option on several occasions, and in each instance my monetary contributions were returned with the following message: *"The Adventist Church does not have a pro-life program."*

I tried the third option for several years without identifying the funds as pro-life funds, and of course, the contributions were gladly accepted. This worked, but left me rather uneasy because my desire was that the funds be used for the benefit of the unborn. This left me with the less desirable option of sending my money to non-Adventist pro-life organizations.

We Need Better Alternatives

 Is this the best I can do? Perhaps yes, but I wish I had the option of sending my pro-life contributions to an Adventist pro-life organization—something that at present does not exist. I wish some Adventists would start a ministry similar to the *"Save the Stork"* entity started not a long time ago. A couple of young individuals designed a very attractive and properly equipped van which they park near abortion clinics, and they offer free sonograms to the women that come for an abortion.

They discovered that instead of angry refusals, their friendly approach works wonders. In one day, they can secure up to fifteen women willing to accept the free sonograms. Those women interested in continuing with the pregnancy are referred to the nearest pregnancy center, which is also free. Many of these women decide to keep their babies until delivery.

A Noble Prospective Ministry

Well, perhaps I am dreaming. If I were younger, I would probably attempt such a project. A van like that costs approximately $ 140,000 dollars, and money is needed to pay for those actually doing the pro-life work. At the present moment, these young men have several vans, and their work is sponsored by pro-life contributions.[229] Why can't we Adventist do something like this instead of profiting from the death of unborn children? Any young volunteers for such a noble mission?

A Stigmata Case in Loma Linda

Some years ago I did write the following allegory as a result of my struggle over what to do with my tithes and offerings. Leading Adventist pro-lifers were leaving Adventism and some of them had decided to move back to Rome because of its strong stand against abortion. This was regrettable, and I thought that there should be other more desirable options. One of said options was to send our money to independent ministries like *"The Quiet Hour," "3ABN," "Amazing Facts,"* and so on. Here is said allegory:

****

"How long have you had these stains on your hands?" My devout Catholic friend inquired. I told him I had noticed them at least a decade ago, and I added that their size and coloration had become more conspicuous with the passage of time, especially on my right hand.

> *"They look to me like a case of stigmata,"* my friend stated with some assurance. *"If I am correct in my assessment, then you might be considered among the most privileged members of Christendom. You might even become a candidate for beatification and even sainthood two or three centuries after you die,"* he added with some excitement. *"I know that your church does not believe in the miracle of stigmata; but, perhaps God is trying to break through to your denomination. You should consult a priest; but first, you might have your doctor analyze these stains to insure they match your own genetic code."*

---

[229] http://www.lifesitenews.com/news/how-some-kids-with-a-van-are-changing-the-pro-life-movement?utm_source=LifeSiteNews.com+Daily+Newsletter&utm_campaign=d2652abd16-LifeSiteNews_com_US_Headlines_03_07_2012&utm_medium=email

The DNA Blood Test Results

My physician ordered, rather reluctantly, a DNA test and a telephone call from my doctor followed. The first question I asked him was whether the test revealed the presence of human blood. He assured me it did. *"But the curious detail,"* he added, *"is that the test reveals the presence of blood from very young individuals. It seems to be either neo-natal or fetal blood. Have you been close, perhaps unawares, to a crime scene?"* He asked.

This turn of events I did not like a bit; nevertheless, making an effort to hide my apprehension, I managed to ask him whether he had heard of similar cases before, to which he responded:

> *"Yes, I have. Especially in the last two decades or so. Actually, I detected an increase of reported cases beginning with the 1973 year. Medical science has been perplexed by this rare phenomenon, and the current theory is that the cause is not physiological, but rather psychological. Science seems to be at a loss trying to explain the presence of foreign bloodstains resulting from exclusively altered psychological mental states. What I recommend is that you see an ethicist, a psychologist, or a psychiatrist."*

Me a mental case? I always thought to be mentally well balanced. This was beyond my psychological pain threshold. I was ready to hang up, but he added the following:

> *"There is a renowned ethics expert who recently published a book designed to help those with this rare symptom. You can see him, or you may want to see your pastor; or, if you are really serious, you may want to consult a well-known psychologist who relocated from Pasadena to Colorado Springs some decades ago; he is the best on this subject. He has written many books on family issues, and he has had a radio show for many years; his name is James Dobson. A trip to his office might be worth the effort. If I were in your shoes, I would consider this!"*

169

The Ethical Diagnosis

Since I dreaded the idea of being diagnosed by a psychiatrist or a psychologist, and since I hated the thought of driving all the way to Colorado, especially in winter, I decided to see my friend, the ethicist. He greeted me with his friendly smile, and put me right at ease with the following words of reassurance:

> *"What you are experiencing should be no cause for worry. This is a quite common situation where symptoms reveal an overactive guilt feeling by association. Your doctor says the DNA test revealed the presence of human blood from a foreign source. We have analyzed this rare phenomenon and we have concluded that it is the blood of non-persons."*

> *"The Holy Book tells us that humans were created in 'God's image" and our prophet assures us that said image represents the 'power to think and to do.' My conclusion is that fetal blood is the blood of an entity that has not developed to a point where we can assign to it the category of personhood. There should not be any guilt associated with such bloodstains. You are as normal as you can be. If you accept this, these blood stains on your hands will eventually, slowly but surely, disappear with time."*

The Verdict of my Pastor

I left the office of my friend greatly relieved, but my problem persisted, so I had no choice but to consult my pastor. His reaction was similar, but slightly different from that of the ethics expert:

> *"Your concern is a valid one. There is something you can do about this problem. You should exercise your rights as a citizen of a democratic country. These bloodstains are the result of a Supreme Court decision rendered back in 1973. As a pastor, I regret the shedding of innocent blood, but the church should respect the freedom God and the government grants to individuals. Remember that Jesus Christ died to make us free. There is nothing more sacred than human freedom, for which our Redeemer paid a high price: his life,"*

"If you cast the right votes, you have no reason to feel guilty for the actions of those whose vote is different from yours. The church must stay out of this controversial issue. We have no right to impose our personal values on those who feel otherwise. Many members of our congregation would feel offended if we were to transfer our guilt feelings upon them on this issue. If you can respect the personal preferences of others, your problem will, slowly but surely, disappear with time."

The Psychologist's Opinion

I hoped against hope that his advice would work for me. The fact is it didn't, and I found myself winding the snowy roads leading to Colorado Springs. The sight of the snow-covered mountain peaks was really impressive, and the fresh and pure air, free from the smog-polluted Southern California landscape, was quite invigorating, which gave me a sense that somehow this trip might help me restore the peace of mind I craved so much. Soon I was in the presence of the renowned psychologist.

"This is definitely not a case of stigmata. Your doctor is correct in stating that these ugly bloodstains have a psychological origin. I also concur with your ethicist belief that humans were created in God's image, and that this image is expressed in our 'power to think and to do.' Nevertheless, this definition of humanness is incomplete. The correct definition includes the 'power to think and to do God's will.' Without that, both Hitler, who exterminated six million innocent Jews, and the Columbine students, who murdered more than a dozen of their classmates, would qualify. They revealed a remarkable 'power to think and to do,' but unfortunately, it was a power to think and to do not God's will, but the will of the Evil One. They had developed the image, not of God, but the image of the one who has been 'a murderer from the beginning.'" "Likewise, I agree with your pastor regarding our duty and privilege to exercise our voting rights."

"Nevertheless, the church has a prophetic role, which is to call people to repentance. Suffering and evil tends to increase whenever the voice of the church is silenced. All it takes for evil to increase is for good people to do nothing. This was true in Germany half a century ago, and it is true today. The Good Book condemns the shedding of innocent blood, and there is no more innocent blood than the blood of the unborn. It also cries to God like the blood of Abel whom Cain murdered."

"Your pastor says that Jesus Christ died to make us free, and I agree. He did die 'to make us free,' but again this sentence is incomplete. He did not offer his life in order to make us free to shed innocent blood, but rather died 'to make us free from sin.' There is a world of difference between these diametrically opposed concepts."

"I also concur with your pastor that abortion is a controversial issue, but your 'Sabbath' is controversial as well, yet your magazines and books and sermons are filled with arguments in favor of worshipping God on the correct day of the week. Your denomination does not keep silent on this issue just because it is controversial."

Listening to all this was almost more than I could bear. My guilt feelings had suddenly increased to the breaking point. I felt like running away from his office without even saying good-bye. Nevertheless, I was somehow glued to the chair I was sitting on. I could not move, and I was almost unable to utter a word either. A long silence followed, after which he made the following final remark

"I noticed that your right hand is the one with the most ugliest blood stains, and I know why this is so. Evidently, you are right handed. Very likely, your right hand is the one that writes the checks to a pro-choice church, which makes you an accomplice in the shedding of all this innocent blood."

The Results of my Research

 On my return to Loma Linda, I went straight to the Heritage section of the Loma Linda University library. I was determined to prove the Colorado Springs psychologist

172

wrong. I searched our church papers for the pro-life articles. The result? A total vacuum, while almost every issue had something about the Sabbath. I said to myself: *"Surely, if I peruse the free-press SDA publications like Adventist Today and Spectrum the result will be different."* It was the same silence about what I now considered also sacred: human life.

I decided to run one more test. It would be my last chance to prove my psychologist wrong. I sent the Lord's money to my church treasurer labeled as *"pro-life/anti-abortion funds."* Four days later they were returned with the incredible explanation that neither the local church nor the Conference had such a program in operation.

This was the last straw, which meant that in the future my tithes and free-will offerings might have to go to some other ministries which are sympathetic to the unborn's right to life or—God forbid—to Rome.

Explanation

I presume you must have guessed that the above parable is merely a way of describing my spiritual struggle over the issue of abortion. I am a second  generation Adventist, and I would never send my tithes and offerings to Rome. Nevertheless, I do admire the Catholic position on abortion. Catholic hospitals do not provide abortion services to their patients while Adventist hospitals do. This is difficult to understand for somebody who for long decades has been indoctrinated in the belief that Adventists do recognize the validity and permanence of the Ten Commandments one of which clearly forbids the killing of innocent human beings.

A Book Every Adventist Should Read[230]

Sometime ago as I was talking with a retired university professor and evangelist whom I greatly admire for his dedication to the Adventist mission,

---

[230] http://adventlife.wordpress.com/2012/02/24/a-book-every-adventist-should-read-by-nic-samojluk/

I was surprised by the following comment he made about the first book I published about Adventism and abortion:[231] *"Every Adventist should read this book."* Was he referring to the Bible? No, since most Adventists are reading or have already read the Bible.

Did he have in mind one of the Ellen White books? Not so, since a great number of Adventists have read quite a bit of what she wrote either directly from one of her books or by reading Adventist material containing some of her quotations. So what book was he referring to? He was talking about a recently published book dealing with the Adventist Church and its new attitude towards abortion.

Since I happen to be the author of said book, I perked my ears, and then decided to crunch some numbers. There are approximately 17 million Adventists in the world, and most of them will not buy my book on their own initiative; which means that I have to give most of them away as a gift. So how much money do I need for such a project?

Approximately 300 million dollars, unless I can find another printer who can provide his service at a much lower price per book. The problem is that I am not rich. I set a very modest fund which has grown a little bit thanks to some generous donors who have read or are reading the book. This has allowed me to give away over 100 copies of the book so far.

So how far am I from my ultimate goal? Well, 17 million minus 140 equals 16,998,060 books to be either sold or given away for free. Do I expect to reach this goal in the few years I have left this side of eternity? Of course not! This reminds me of a Latin proverb which states: *"Pedes in terra et sidera visus"* [The feet on the ground and the sight at the stars].

A more modest goal would be what a renowned retired LLU ethics professor told me: *"This book should be in every Adventist school library."* Either way, the goal is beyond my limited financial means, but the Lord is rich and he can provide the means to reach either of those two objectives.

---

[231] "From Pro-life to Pro Choice," http://www.lulu.com/shop/search.ep?type=&keyWords=nic+samojluk&sitesearch=lulu.com& q=&x=12&y=12. The book can also be ordered from Amazon.

Perhaps you have read what some critics have written about my book. Here is a sample for you to consider. The following was taken from the printer's page where the book is advertised for sale to the public.

Jan. 10, 2012

By Michael Senseney

"In the early 90s, as an Elder in my SDA church, I corresponded with the presidents of the Columbia Union and the General Conference on the issue of abortions being performed in Maryland Adventist hospitals. At first, the Union president attempted to assure me that I was taken in by vicious rumors. I obtained statistics that showed thousands of abortions were being performed bringing in millions of dollars. When the facts were presented to SDA leadership, the correspondence ended with nothing but the silent ignoring of my pleas. Unfortunately this appears to be the standard operating procedure utilized by church leadership toward any and all pro-life Adventists. Nic Samojluk's book reveals..."

Jan. 17, 2012
By Teresa

"Most Seventh-day Adventists attempt to balance a pro-life moral stance while at the same time being legally pro-choice. They fear legislation against abortion would somehow begin the process of infringing upon their religious rights. Yet, it was not always so. Mr. Samojluk meticulously records how their church so drastically evolved from passionately protective of the unborn life in the SDA pioneer days to today's liberal policies.

This is not a vitriolic anti-SDA exposé, but a ardent faithful church member who is called by God to cry out for the unborn. And for those of us who are not Adventist, we urge you as a denomination to recognize how it appears to Christianity when you claim..."

☆☆☆☆☆ [no rating]

175

Jan. 18, 2012
By John Stevens, Sr

"I have corresponded for years with this author and unfortunately he has shared misinformation. There is no statement ever made by Ellen White about abortion or opposition to it. Those are mere inaccurate assertions. In a court of law they would be thrown out. Her husband, James, who was not a prophet like Ellen, was opposed to it and John Harvey Kellogg, a pantheist in his latter days believed it was a living person, a murder to abort. Of course the Bible does not forbid killing but does forbid murder, which has hatred, contrary to love, as the motive. Of course all of nature is viewed unbiblical by pantheists, which see God in all and accept all to be gods. Pan is many, theism is gods.

The official church position has always been prochoice but became more conservative under Bob Folkenburg but it is not forbidden. The Bible does not have any sanctions against abortion even though there are 105 capital punishment crimes. The fetus has borrowed life from the mother and becomes a living person upon birth and independent breathing. Adam was not a living person until he breathed. The popular opposition to abortion came into Christianity through paganism based on the first life in the Bible when Satan told Eve, "You shall not surely die," the foundation for the unbiblical teaching of the natural immortality of the soul. Pagans executed those who aborted in Egypt and Canaan but at Mt Sinai God placed not one restriction against abortion. In fact in Numbers 5 the trial of jealous he commanded for a woman suspected to be pregnant form infidelity but not caught.

If she were guilty God performed a supernatural abortion on her as a penalty. Egyptians ordered the Jewish mothers of baby boys to drown them. So much for the much acclaimed sanctity of life by some of those who are devotees of anti abortion. They are the same ones that will not support tax funding to help women with babies and no income to get financial help. The pagan practice of worshipping the fetus and then killing the baby once it is born if it is undesirable has infiltrated professed Christianity. I have published a book on the subject. The Bible and God are both pro life and pro choice, but independent life comes after birth. The mother is the most

176

miraculous life support system ever, even beyond our imagination."

 [no rating]

Jan. 18, 2012
By Nic Samojluk

"John Stevens, Sr. is right in his claim that Ellen White did never use the word abortion in her prolific writings. Nevertheless, she did make a clear reference to the almost murder of unborn children. If neglecting the health of a pregnant woman was almost murdering the unborn for Ellen White, can we logically conclude that Ellen was neutral regarding the actual killing of an unborn baby? Here is what she said:

> *"If the father would become acquainted with physical law, he might better understand his obligations and responsibilities. He would see that he had been guilty of almost murdering his children, by suffering so many burdens to come upon the mother, compelling her to labor beyond..."*

★★★★★

Nov. 22, 2011
By Tammy_Roesch

"Thank you Nic, for documenting all this information! If anyone wants the facts as to where the SDA Church, as a Denomination, REALLY stands on the subject of Abortion, they should read this book. There will be no true "Revival & Reformation" in the Church, while the SDA Church is on the Pro-Choice side of the aisle. There are ONLY two sides....there is no "FENCE" to sit on, no "middle of the road" to walk on, when it comes to the subject of Abortion. I hope and pray that enough people will read this book and demand that the Church take the side of LIFE and not DEATH. God bless you, Nic!"

★★★★★

Nov. 12, 2011
By Martin Weber

 *"Nic has written an important book for Seventh-day Adventists on what may be the greatest moral issue of our time. What I've read of it is very impressive. I wish Adventists everywhere had the integrity that Orlando-based Adventist Health System has when it comes to unborn human life (hospitals in the Southeast U.S. and Mid-America). Concern to protect unborn human life should be at the top of our list in the current quest for revival and reformation."*

★★★★★

Nov. 28, 2011
By Juanita Y. Mayes

"This book is a very interesting read for every Adventist church member who cares about the cause of life and the sanctity of human life. The reader may be shocked and saddened by the information shared in its pages. Our Adventist pioneers, including James and Ellen White would feel the same way; for they too, were passionately pro life and supported the efforts in their day to make abortion illegal.

I also was shocked and saddened about our Adventist leaders and pastors whose opinion prevailed, resulting in our church's turning to the pro choice side of the abortion issue. Read how in one hospital, the decision makers decided to allow elective abortion rather than to trust God to bless and prosper them for remaining true to the Ten Commandments. Learn the reasons why our leaders and pastors took the positions they did and came to side with pro choice position rather than pro-life one. One article I have in mind that is included in the book did not even seem to be authored by a Christian person.

Perhaps the time is now for the SDA church to go back to our beginnings and get back on the path of the pioneers and follow on it. Maybe this book is written for such a time as this. This book is a must read for every Seventh Day Adventist church member, pastor, and leader. Find out why we must defend the right to life of our little brothers and sisters, the smallest and youngest members in God's family."

Why Some Adventists Left the Church

You might be aware that 1992 was the year the General Conference Autumn Council of the Adventist Church approved a document known as the *"Guidelines on Abortion,"* which redefined the original and true meaning of the Commandment which forbids the killing of innocent human beings.

Several pro-life leading members of the church decided they could no longer identify themselves with and support a religious organization that had compromised on a fundamental moral issue like the killing of innocent unborn babies.

Some started independent ministries, one of them joined the Jewish orthodox faith, and several others decided to go back to Rome because of the strong pro-life position on abortion of the Catholic Church.

What follows is the testimony of one of them who could no longer belong to a church that had compromised with evil and began profiting from the death of human beings.

 Beverly Whelton, a member of the SDA church, became dissatisfied with the pro-choice position of the church and unable to continue worshipping with SDAs since she felt that doing so would imply endorsing its beliefs. She left Adventism and later on joined the Catholic Church.

This experience was traumatic for her, and she wrote several letters to her relatives explaining to them the reasons for her action. In those letters, she clarified that her love for Jesus had not diminished when she left the SDA church, and that she found peace of mind within the Catholic communion. Here is how she explained her experience:[232]

---

[232] Beverly Whelton, "A Woman of Letters" *Envoy* (Mar./Apr. 1999).

"As you know, over the last several years, I found myself unable to worship within the Seventh Day Adventist setting. Their anti-intellectual attitude turned me off, in addition to their pro-choice position on abortion (communicated in the church paper, Review and Harold [sic], October 1992).

While I rejected the Adventist faith, I nevertheless loved Jesus very much. My heart ached to go to a church, but I wouldn't step into a house of worship unless I could be sure they had the full truth. When you worship in a church, you're endorsing the beliefs of that body, and I couldn't do that if I wasn't sure those beliefs were right.

Jeanette, I'd cry and cry and beg God to let me know the truth. I'd always pray the Lord's Prayer – sometimes that was all I could pray. In my mind, I imagined Jesus on the cross, and I called out to Him. But I couldn't go to church, because I didn't know how to worship this beautiful God as He deserved. (Hear the pain and tears; I'm crying.) I knew Jesus must be worshipped in truth and holiness, but I didn't know how."

On April 11, 1993, I entered the Catholic Church, becoming a part of His very Body. Since then, I've finally known the joy of God-given worship. My Christ has continued to guide my life, and I will always rejoice in His Presence. Where the Eucharist is, He is. And where He is, I must be."

SMOKE & MIRRORS

Mind If I Smoke?

Loma Linda University has been in the forefront in the fight against the smoking habit, which kills approximately 420,000 Americans every year. It is a noble work, which has in the past received the support of both the government and the general public, and forced even the manufacturers of tobacco products to join in the efforts to warn the public about the deleterious effects of the smoking addiction.

Many scientists have discovered unique methods designed to help those wishing to quit smoking for good, including Linda Hyder Ferry, also known as Dr. Hope, who was able to identify a stimulant antidepressant named buprorion, which possesses the ability of duplicating the effects of nicotine on the brain, thus making quitting the habit less painful. Research has demonstrated that those who stop smoking, have the chance of extending their lives by four or five years on the average, and avoid serious illnesses.

Choose Life

My question is: If it pays to extend the life of a person by four or five years, how about extending the life of a human being by an entire life span? Every year 420,000 dye from smoking-related diseases, but a million and a half human beings are killed by abortion. Stopping an abortion does extend the life of a human being not by four or five years, but rather by a lifetime. Shouldn't society do something about this? We did away with slavery over a century ago. Can't we do away with abortion as well?

Odds of dying of Any Cause

As I was leafing through the August 2006 copy of the *National Geographic Magazine* I noticed the statistics showing the odds of dying of any cause in the United States. The odds are as follows in descending order:

Heart disease: 1 in 5
Cancer: 1 in 7
Stroke: 1 in 24
Motor vehicle accident: 1 in 84
Suicide: 1 in 119
Falling: 1 in 218
Firearm assault: 1 in 314
Pedestrian accident: 1 in 626
Drowning: 1 in 1,008
Motorcycle accident: 1 in 1,020
Fire or smoke: 1 in 1,113
Bicycling accident: 1 in 4,919
Air/space accident: 1 in 5,051
Accidental firearm discharge: 1 in 5,134
Accidental electrocution: 1 in 9,968
Alcohol poisoning: 1 in 10,048
Hot weather: 1 in 13,729
Hornet wasp, or bee sting: 1 in 56,789
Legal execution: 1 in 62,468
Lightning: 1 in 79,746
Earthquake: 1 in 117,127
Flood: 1 in 144,156
Fireworks discharge: 1 in 340,733

What I noticed also is that the odds of dying as a result of an abortion was missing from the report. This prompted me to send the following comment by E-mail to the magazine:

> *"While leafing through the latest issue of your magazine I noticed that your statistics showing the odds of dying of any cause in the U.S. is 1 in 5 for heart disease, 1 in 7 for cancer, 1 in 24 for stroke, and so on. How about the odds of dying of abortion? I read elsewhere that it is 1 in 3. If that is correct, then the highest cause of death would be abortion instead of heart disease.*

> *Is your omission due to accident or design? Are not the unborn members of the human race? Most abortions are performed when there is a beating heart, brain waves, a torso, hands and feet. Isn't this sufficient evidence that the unborn are in fact human beings? Shouldn't their deaths [1.5 million per year] be included in the statistics?"*

This is 2014, and I am still waiting for a response from the ***National Geographic Magazine***

A Corporate Apology from the German and Austrian SDA Church[233]

It is a well-known fact that the late John Paul II did apologize for the past sins of the church, not once, but on numerous occasions. According to one reporter, he did so over a hundred times. Do you think that the current church leaders have a moral obligation to confess the sins of those who preceded them in church office? Evidently the officers of the German and Austrian Seventh-day Adventist church think so, since they did publicly apologize for the Adventist Church departure from moral duty during the Nazi regime. Here is the evidence

> *"Noting the sixtieth anniversary of the end of World War II, Seventh-day Adventist church leaders in Germany and Austria have released a declaration saying they "deeply regret" any participation in or support of Nazi activities during the war. The church bodies "honestly confess" a failure "in following our Lord" by not protecting Jews, and others, from that era's genocide, widely known as the Holocaust.*

---

[233] Mark A. Kellner, "German and Austrian Churches Apologize for Holocaust Actions" *Adventist Review/Adventist news* (2006).

Millions of people perished from war atrocities, including more than 6 million Jews who were exterminated in Nazi persecutions during the 12-year period of 1933 to 1945

The church says it also regrets "that in some of our publications . . . there were found articles glorifying Adolf Hitler and agreeing with the ideology of anti-Semitism in a way that is unbelievable from today's [perspective].

Church leaders also expressed regret that "our peoples became associated with racial fanaticism destroying the lives and freedom of 6 million Jews and representatives of minorities in all of Europe" and "that many Seventh-day Adventists did not share the need and suffering of their Jewish fellow-citizens.

Under various racial decrees, some Adventist congregations expelled members of Jewish heritage. One, Max-Israel Munk, was placed in two concentration camps by the Nazis and survived and returned to his church after the war. He said he did not wish to act toward his congregation in the way in which he had been treated, according to Daniel Heinz, a church archivist at Friedensau Adventist University who has studied Adventist activities during the National Socialist era. ...

During World War I a portion of the German Adventist church had split off, opposing any military service. This led the National Socialists in 1936 to ban the so-called "Reform Movement" during their time in power. Brugger said concern over a Nazi closure of the main Adventist churches may have weighed on leaders in that era. ... "

 As I read and re-read this official report by the church, I wondered: Will the SDA church some day issue a similar apology for not actively opposing the genocide that has been taking place since the legalization of abortion in the U.S. back in 1973? We have used tons of ink and paper decrying the desecration of God's Holy Time–the Sabbath. We feel it is a great offense against the God of heaven when we break the Fourth Commandment of the Decalogue. Well, how about the other commandment that reads: You shall not murder? If time is sacred, how about human life? Is the death of over 50 million innocent babies less offensive to the Lord than worshipping God on the wrong day of the week?

The current merciless slaughter of innocent children before they are born reminds me of the murder of innocent Jewish boys by King Pharaoh of old and the slaughter of the innocents by King Herod. The church has apologized for keeping silence while six million innocent Jews were exterminated in the Nazi concentration camps. Do you think that the day may come when the future leaders of the General Conference may offer a similar apology for doing nothing while the murder of the children through abortion was taking place in America and the world? If you think I am on the right track, don't you think that it would be much better to do the right thing today?

A Sure Way of Preserving Women's Abortion Rights

Following Senator Dianne Feinstein unsuccessful efforts to block the confirmation of Judge Alito to the U.S. Supreme Court some years ago, I decided to contact the California Senator with a suggestion regarding a sure way Democrats could succeed in preserving women's right to choose in the future. Here is a copy of my E-mail to her.

"Dear Senator Dianne Feinstein,

Considering the Democratic failure to stop the confirmation of Judge Alito for the U.S. Supreme Court, I would like to suggest a sure way of protecting women's right to abortion in the future.

It is a well-known fact that children tend to inherit the values of their parents. This means that the children of Pro-choice women will likely inherit the Pro-choice values of their parents, and they will be the ones who will fight to preserve women's abortion rights in the future. The problem is that we are killing them by the thousands.

We have killed 47 million of those who would have likely defended the right of women to choose. We need to reverse this trend if we want to succeed in protecting women's rights. Democrats like you need to wield their influence to reduce the number of abortions. Otherwise, the number of Pro-choice individuals will continue to decrease, while the number of Pro-life will keep increasing, since Pro-life women do not abort theirs. This is precisely why the Pro-life movement is gaining strength.

Were it not for both the legal and illegal immigration, our U.S. population would slowly implode. We need to reverse this trend, and one way of accomplishing this is by reducing the number of abortions. The security of out country demands that we remedy this situation. We need to better control our borders, reduce the number of illegal immigrants, and increase the birth rate of Americans. Anything you can do encourage the decrease of the number of abortions in our country will help us in achieving these objectives.

There is more. Surveys have discovered that in France out of three babies born, one of them is born to a Moslem woman. At this trend, Europe will be increasingly populated by Moslems. Decreasing the number of abortions by non-Moslems can reverse this trend. If we want to continue to lead the world, we need to set a wise example to follow by other nations. In the U.S., the birth rate is well below what is needed to maintain a stable demographic level. It is imperative that we take steps to reverse this undesirable trend. Can we count on you to support the pro-life agenda in the future?"

 This took place many years ago; needless to say, my efforts to entice Senator Feinstein to embrace the pro-life program did not succeed; and to all appearances, no amount of scientific evidence showing the deleterious effects of the legalization of abortion will change her determined and obstinate attitude in defense of the killings of innocent pre-born human beings.

THE DEATH OF ABORTION

When Does Human Life Begin?

What We Seem to Know

 We Seventh-day Adventists pride ourselves in having an answer for almost any doctrinal question, because we see ourselves as the prophetical church with the last message for a perishing world. We know the correct day for worship, we know why health is important, we know how to identify the antichrist, we claim to know the exact date when Jesus Christ moved from the Holy Place to the Most Holy in the heavenly sanctuary, and we know what will determine the final destiny of those who claim to be Christ's followers.

What We Prefer to Ignore

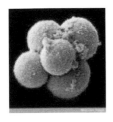 We seem to have an answer to all the most important life and death questions ever posed by human beings. Nevertheless, there is one basic question we do not have an answer for, and that is: When does human life begin? This is rather strange, because we used to know the answer for such a question, but it seems like we have decided to forget what the answer was, and this happened shortly after the controversial discussion about human cloning took place some years ago. Perhaps you are wondering whether I am making this up. Look at the following declaration by a highly respected leader of our church:[234]

---

[234] Bettina Krause. "ANN Feature: Broader Religious Input Needed in Stem Cell Debate, Says Adventist Ethicist" *Adventist News network/ Seventh-day Adventist Church* (7 Aug. 2001).

> *"The church has chosen not to define the precise moment human life begins–a moment science finds difficult to pinpoint."*

What Others Do Know

 What surprises me is the fact that members of other religious denominations that do not claim to be the last prophetic movement before Christ's return to this earth do know that human life begins at conception. I am thinking about the Southern Baptists who have such a statement among their fundamental doctrinal beliefs. Even the Pope of Rome, whom we have described in the past as the biblical Antichrist, also knows when human life begins; and not only knows this fundamental biological fact, but he is also adamant in the defense of the unborn.

And I want to add another group of people: the political leaders of South Dakota, who have some years ago made such a declaration when they voted on a new law making it illegal for women to have an abortion, except in the case when the life of the pregnant woman is at risk and the physician feels saving the lives of both the woman and the baby is impossible. Note the following statement:[235]

> *"The South Dakota bill declares "that life begins at the time of conception" and "that to fully protect the rights, interests, and health of the pregnant mother, the rights, interest, and life of her unborn child, and the mother's fundamental natural intrinsic right to a relationship with her child, abortions in South Dakota should be prohibited." ..."*

---

[235] Michael Williams "South Dakota: Life Begins At Conception" *Michael Williams* (11 Feb. 2004).

Aren't We God's Remnant?

 My question is: How can we dare to claim to be the prophetic Remnant people of God on earth, having the last message for a perishing world, if we ignore this fundamental truth: that human life begins at conception? We are right in declaring to the world that God's Holy Time–the Sabbath–is sacred; but is human life not sacred as well? We do know the limits of sacred time, we know exactly when the sacred hours of the Sabbath begin: at sun down, but we claim to ignore when human life begins. How can we justify this ignorance?

The Need to Know the Limits of Human Life

 We do declare that human life is precious in the eyes of God, and that human life should be protected, but how can human life be properly protected if we declare to the whole world that we do not know when human life begins?

Would it make sense for the president of the U.S. to assert that our borders should be protected, and then add that we do not know the exact location of those borders? Would it make sense for our government to order our border patrol agents to secure our borders, and then admit that we do not know where those borders lie? How can we then assert that human life should be protected from its inception and then admit that we do not know when human life begins?

We Failed in Nazi Germany

 Some years ago the SDA leaders of both Austria and Germany issued a joint declaration apologizing for the church's silence and cooperation with Hitler when the genocide of six million Jews was taking place in Germany during the Nazi regime. By declaring that we do not know when human life begins, are we not endorsing the slaughter of the innocent again, this time the genocide of the unborn? Wouldn't it be better to position ourselves definitely within the Pro-life camp, instead of wavering on the sidelines?

189

Our Deafening Silence on the Abortion Issue

 Why are we silent on this life and death issue? When was the last time you heard a sermon on this subject, or read an article in our magazines condemning the slaughter of the innocents? When we hear the deafening silence of our church on the issue of abortion, can't we foresee that we are preparing the way for future SDA leaders for a similar apology sometime in the coming years?

Shouldn't we wake up and take a decided stand against this horrendous practice that has since 1973 decimated our population by 56 million victims? Can't we see what is taking place in our own country?\

Freedom to the Iraqis and Afghanistanies but Death to our Own Children

 While we are liberating the Iraqis and Afghanistanies from decades of oppression, we are blind to the fact that our own children are being mercilessly slaughtered in our own backyard and in our own Adventist hospitals.

We send our soldiers to protect foreigners from terrorism, but at the same time we do not have the courage to protect our own children from a sure death! We spend billions of dollars to secure the future of foreigners, but fail to secure the future of our own! We try to police the world, while failing to police our own country. What happened to us? Have we lost our moral compass?

Aren't We a Prophetic Movement?

 If our church is truly a prophetic movement destined to warn the world about the approaching Day of Judgment, then we can't ignore the fact that God does care for the life of the most innocent members of humanity: the unborn. The one who said, Let the children come to me, will not overlook our actions if we persist in looking the other way while the

190

unborn are being led to the slaughter house. How can those children come to Jesus, if we deprive them of life before they have a chance to take their first breath?

The Death of Abortion

For several years I published a web page entitled SDA Forum, which eventually metamorphosed into the current web page I still publish under the following name: Advent Life.[236] It generated a reasonable number of visitors and readers. Some of the articles I published in it were long, while others were rather short. I still remember the shortest one of them which surprised me because of the number of readers it attracted: 3696. I want to share it with you. This is what I wrote:

> *"Abortion carries the seeds of its own demise. It is a well-known fact that children tend to inherit the values of their parents. This means that, if pro-choicers kill their children, while pro-lifers do not, eventually pro-choicers are doomed to extinction."*

I am indebted for this idea to an article I read which carried said title published by *The Covenant News*, and here is the paragraph that inspired me with the notion that abortion carries the seeds of its own destruction.[237]

> *"Abortion and birth control are antagonistic to Creation. They waste under their own curse as they course toward self-destruction. They leave in their wake the deaths of individuals, the destruction of families, a void in communities, and the downfall of nations. They rip, slash and tear at the moral fabric of a religious people."*

---

[236] http://adventlife.wordpress.com
[237] Dan Holman, "The Death of Abortion" *The Covenant News* (28 Feb. 2006). http://www.covenantnews.com/holman060228.htm

The Most Dangerous Place on Earth

Introduction

I need to clarify that I wrote the following short item several years ago, when George Bush was in the White House. I am including it in this book because I believe that it's applicable to the current situation in our country and elsewhere in the world:

On the Brink of Nuclear War

Considering the fact that both Pakistan and India do possess nuclear weapons of mass destruction, and given the unequal confrontation between a giant and a pigmy, as far as both population and number of soldiers each has at its disposal, CNN correspondent Wolf Blitzer, has recently described the disputed territory of Kashmir between India and Pakistan as *"The Most Dangerous Place on Earth"* at the present moment.

This politically precarious situation represents an issue of grave concern for the Bush administration, because in the event of a nuclear exchange between the two countries, the lives of millions of innocent civilians would be in jeopardy, and our own American soldiers operating in Afghanistan and Pakistan would be at great risk. The situation is so serious, that President Bush has decided to send Secretary Rumsfeld as his personal envoy with the difficult mission of trying to diffuse the tension between the two countries.

The Most Dangerous Place on Earth

I grant the fact that Kashmir is an extremely dangerous place on earth right now; nevertheless, I am convinced that the most dangerous place on earth today is not Kashmir, but rather being inside the womb as an unborn. This is the place where a human being runs the greatest risk of being either poisoned or dismembered before he/she has a chance of seeing the light of day for the first time in his/her life.

Who Has the Right to Live?

Since the dawn of humanity people have debated the question dealing with the right to life. In the Old Testament, murderers, prostitutes, sorcerers, and Sabbath breakers had no right to live. Moses declared that they had to be stoned to death, and some of them suffered such penalty.

 Nevertheless, when Jesus was confronted with the dilemma of what to do with the woman caught in adultery, he declared: *"Whoever is without sin, let him throw the first stone."* Well, you know what happened, as the Master knelt down to write on the sand, one by one the woman's accusers left, and then Jesus said to her: *"Neither do I condemn thee, go and sin no more."*

Throughout history, only a selected group of people had the right to live. They were called free men. Slaves had no such right.

A master could kill his slave with impunity, and many did so; but then came Abraham Lincoln, and decided that fighting a civil war was worth the effort to free slaves from this injustice.

When the American Civil War was over, slaves suddenly became members of humanity with certain rights, including the right to life.

 This right to life is embedded in the Declaration of Independence and the Fourteenth Amendment of the U.S. Constitution. In 1973, Nine Unelected Justices of the U.S. Supreme Court decided to ignore this fundamental right by fabricating out of thin air the alleged right to choose—to kill, of course—innocent unborn babies prior to their birth.

Let us examine what these documents declare regarding the right to life. Do they include the right to deny the right to be born once a human life has been created and developing inside the womb of a woman?[238]

---

[238] College of Law. U.S. Historical Documents: "Declaration of Independence" (n.d.). http://www.law.ou.edu/hist/decind.html

> *"We hold these Truths to be self-evident, that all Men are created equal, that they are endowed by their Creator with certain unalienable Rights, that among these are Life, Liberty and the Pursuit of Happiness — That to secure these Rights, Governments are instituted among Men, deriving their just Powers from the Consent of the Governed, that whenever any Form of Government becomes destructive to these Ends, it is the Right of the People to alter or to abolish it, and to institute new Government, laying its Foundation on such Principles and organizing its Powers in such Form, as to them shall seem most likely to effect their Safety and Happiness."*

Now let's take a look at the Fourteenth Amendment to the U.S. Constitution:[239]

> *"Section 1. All persons born or naturalized in the United States, and subject to the jurisdiction thereof, are citizens of the United States and of the state wherein they reside. No state shall make or enforce any law which shall abridge the privileges or immunities of citizens of the United States; nor shall any state deprive any person of life, liberty, or property, without due process of law; nor deny to any person within its jurisdiction the equal protection of the laws."*

 If you read carefully the above-quoted statement, you will realize that in order to be entitled to life, you must have been born within the territory of the United States, or else become a naturalized citizen. On the surface, it seems to imply that the unborn are not entitled to life. Nevertheless, if we say this, then we must also conclude that non-citizens are also deprived of the protection granted to citizens.

---

[239] Cornell Law School, "United States Constitution: Amendment XIV" (n.d.). http://www.archives.gov/exhibits/charters/constitution_amendments_11-27.html. If the law protects the lives of immigrants who were not born in the U.S., fairness requires that the lives of the unborn should be protected likewise.

Is this the case? Am I free to murder those who have entered illegally into the U.S. territory, or those who have not yet become citizens? I do not think so! The law protects them, even though they were neither born on U.S. soil, nor have they yet become naturalized citizens of the country.

If this is true, then I conclude that those who are waiting to be born should have the same right to life and the protection of U.S. law. Do they? Why not? The answer lies in the erroneous thinking of nine Justices of the U.S. Supreme Court who four decades ago decided to deprive the unborn of their unalienable right to life. What kind of reasoning did lead them to make such an unwarranted conclusion? The answer is simple: they invented the right to murder the innocent out of the right to privacy.

My question is: can my right to privacy include the right to deprive another human being of life? Is my privacy more sacred than the right to life of those who are waiting to be born? Can this right to freedom truncate somebody else's right to life? The violation of my right to privacy can represent a temporary inconvenience, while the right to life, once taken, cannot be given back. The result of this loss is irreversible. Doesn't common sense dictate that the right to life should have priority over any other rights? Is my thinking on this matter morally unbalanced?

If not, then I conclude that those nine judges who removed the unborn's right to life are guilty of one of the most serious blunders in U.S. history, and it is time to make the proper correction! We need another Abraham Lincoln who is willing to stand for the rights of those who were declared non-persons four decades ago, and thus became easy prey of abortionists whose aim is profit from the genocide of the unborn.

My fellow Adventist believers, we need to stop profiting from the killing of innocent unborn children, a practice that started back in 1970 in the state of Hawaii and spread to several other Adventist medical institutions. We need to join the pro-life movement! We have traditionally identified ourselves as those who keep the Ten Commandment, yet we have been breaking one the them with impunity. This cannot continue! We must repent of this evil.

The Right to Kill

A. Killing the Guilty

Some years ago the then U.S. Attorney General John Ashcroft announced that he might *"consider seeking the death penalty for Robert Hansen, a former FBI agent"* charged with the crime of passing extremely sensitive documents to Russia. Did Ashcroft have the right to take the life of another human being? As an individual, he did not possess said right, but, invested with the authority society had granted him, he did have the legal right to seek this *"ultimate sanction"* against one who had compromised the security of our American personnel, whose life might have been placed in jeopardy as a result of said treasonous action. [240]

Of course, there are those who are adamantly opposed to the death penalty because of its finality, and the undeniable risk of executing an individual who later on might be discovered to have been innocent of the crime. Actually, there have been a large number of reported cases of individuals whose innocence was discovered after decades of incarceration. The technological advances in DNA testing have proved very useful in exonerating many prisoners who otherwise would have ended their life behind bars.

As I was surfing the Internet searching for specific examples, I stumbled on several cases that took place in the State of Texas, including that of Christopher Ochoa, who admitted the killing out of fear for his life, Todd Robinson, who was pardoned by Gov. George W. Bush, and Roy Criner, who was wrongly sentenced to 99 years in prison for a crime he did not commit. This brings us to another notorious case:

Timothy McVeigh, who managed to level the Alfred P. Murrah Federal Building solo style, in which 168 totally innocent people died, including 19 children, and for which action Timothy has shown not the slightest sign of remorse. When he was scheduled to die, Attorney General John Ashcroft

---

[240] http://adventlife.wordpress.com/2012/02/12/the-right-to-kill-by-nic-samojluk/

postponed his execution as a result of the FBI failure to turn more than 3,000 pages of documents to McVeigh's lawyers during the trial.

 Would you question society's right to end the life of one who cowardly destroyed the lives of 168 innocent people? Most Americans are in favor of the death penalty when the guilt of murderers is unquestionable. Nevertheless, there are those who were opposed to the execution of McVeigh for many reasons: it does not right the wrong, it shows that society believes in the use of violence, it grants him what he wishes for–notoriety and death– and it diminishes our respect for the sacredness of human life.

Cardinal Roger Mahony, the former Catholic Archbishop of Los Angeles, added another reason for sparing the life of Timothy McVeigh: providing him with prison time to increase the chance that he might one day realize the enormity of his crime.

B. Killing the Innocent

Regardless of what society thinks about the execution of criminals whose guilt leaves no room for doubt, there is a universal agreement that innocent individuals do not deserve to die–much less for the crime that someone else has committed. Even McVeigh admitted that, had he known that there were children in the Oklahoma federal building, he might have reconsidered his terrorist plan. I used to support the capital punishment as a useful deterrent of crime, but I changed my mind when I read the reported cases of a large number of individuals who had been incarcerated for crimes they did not commit, and after the execution of Karla Faye Tucker, who experienced a conversion while in prison, and who showed more than anybody else that she was no longer a threat to society.

 The finality and irreversibility of this type of punishment makes me wonder about the wisdom of insisting on a remedy which does not provide for redress in the event of an erroneous verdict. For this reason, I concur with the suggestion of Pope John Paul II in his *"Evangelium Vitae"* encyclical that the death penalty should probably be *"abolished completely."* It is true, that there might be cases where the

likelihood of making an error in judgment is probably zero, and the McVeigh case is a good example; nevertheless, isn't it better to leave the imposition of the death penalty to the only one who is infallible in his judgment: Almighty God, the only one who can redress the wrong in the event of a mistake someone else has committed. Even McVeigh admitted that,

D. Killing the Unborn

If you agree with me that it is a miscarriage of justice to take the life of an innocent individual, then you probably would also concur with me that either dismembering or poisoning the unborn represent an act of cruelty and unfairness, since it would be hard to suggest that an unborn baby could be guilty of any crime. This is why The Catholic Bishops of New York State issued the following statement some years ago:

> *"The death penalty is no more the answer to crime than abortion is the answer for unplanned pregnancies. Death is never the answer."*

Why is it then that we have sacrificed over fifty million unborn babies since 1973? For the simple reason that the Supreme Court, with the stroke of a pen, deprived the unborn of personhood, leaving them at the mercy of the pregnant woman and her physician.

Since then, some abortionists have discovered that the art of killing can be much more lucrative than the art of healing, for which they were originally trained, since they can collect a fee for the abortion, and another from the sale of baby parts. One of them, Dr. Edward C. Allred, former owner of 21 abortion clinics in California, has been described as mass delivering aborted babies the way McDonald restaurants turns hamburgers.

Having started with a *"negative net worth"* back in 1967, three years after graduating from Loma Linda University; he eventually, thanks to his expertise in delivering dead babies, became a *"horse-racing magnate"* that traveled with a *"16-member security force"* as protection from anti-abortion zealots. He has contributed through his many business entities\ nearly half a million dollars to many Republican candidates, including Pete Wilson, Matt Fong, and others, many of whom were declared *"anti-abortion"* politicians.

He seemed to be insulated from criticism by the media, as discovered by a pro-lifer who accidentally found out that he was in court testifying in his own behalf at the Orange County Superior Court. He immediately notified the Orange County Register, the Los Angeles Times, and other smaller papers, who refused to report the news. This *"mega-abortionist"* settled the wrongful death of the Hispanic woman in a hurry.

Some years ago, before he retired and sold his business to a Redlands, California dentist, Dr. Allred sued Planned Parenthood *"for taking away a lucrative contract to do abortions for Kaiser HMO,"* but his hopes of obtaining an injunction against the competitor of his Family Planning Associates failed, and he had no choice but to settle the lawsuit.

Stopping the Killing

 You may wonder what it would take to stop this merciless killing of the innocent. It all hinges on the way society defines personhood. Back in 1973 the U.S. Supreme Court determined that the unborn were divested of personhood, and consequently not entitled to the protection of the law. Since then, the war between pro-abortion and pro-life forces has been raging on without abatement.

Some years ago the *"Arkansas Supreme Court ruled that a fetus is a person,"* thus reversing a lower court decision. The case involved the wrongful death of a woman and her 12 week fetus, both of whom died due to negligent medical care.

It is not difficult to guess what the outcome will be if there is an appeal to the U.S. Supreme Court! I would invite you to decide for yourself whether the Arkansas Supreme Court were right in their decision.

You can do this by looking at the picture-shot during surgery-of a tiny hand of a *"21-week-old unborn named Samuel Alexander Armas,"*[241] diagnosed with spina bifida. If you agree with me that said tiny hand reaching for the hand of the surgeon represents a person, instead of a mere lump of tissue, then what shall we say regarding the late abortions?

Not long ago, a woman was sentenced to 12 years in prison in South Carolina for using *"crack cocaine during pregnancy,"* which caused the death of her unborn child. You don't punish somebody for killing a lump of cells in your body!

The title of this article is *"The Right to Kill."* Do you think that women have an innate right to kill their children before they are born? Do you think that husbands and boyfriends have the right to demand the death of the unborn if the pregnancy was unplanned?

Evidently Robert Blake, the notorious Hollywood actor, was convinced that he was right when he bitterly complained to Bonny Lee Bakley, his wife, prior to her murder: *"You swore to me, you promised ...'I will have an abortion' ... and that was a lie ... a big lie. That's the kind of lie that God looks down and says 'Hey, wait a minute.'"*

We do not know who murdered Bakley, but her husband became the prime and only suspect overnight. Did he hire a hit man to murder his wife because she refused to have an abortion? We do not know, but there is no doubt that he felt he had the right to demand the killing of her daughter. What is the difference between hiring a hit man to kill somebody and hiring a licensed abortionist to do the same? If you hire a hit man, you go to jail, but if you hire an abortionist, both you and the physician are protected by a twisted legal system. May the Lord have mercy on us!

---

[241] http://www.snopes.com/photos/medical/thehand.asp

200

The God Given Right to Choose

 After years of blogging with Adventists on a variety of forums about abortion, I have discovered that no matter what argument I use in defense of the unborn's right to life, those who oppose my views end with the following entrenched position: *"Abortion is wrong, but women should have the right to choose!"* So let me see if we can apply the same policy to other areas of our moral behavior:

1. Rape is wrong, but men should have the right to choose!

2. Sexual abuse of children is wrong but men should have the right to choose!

3. Burglary is wrong, but men should have the right to choose!

4. Terrorism is wrong, but men should have the right to choose!

5. Slavery is wrong, but men should have the right to choose!

6. Homicide is wrong, but men should have the right to choose!

7. Genocide is wrong, but men should have the right to choose!

Here is my question: If you agree that all the above described moral actions which cause harm to other human beings are wrong and must we punished, why do we insist that in the case of abortion, women should have the right to kill their own children with impunity?

Why is this a sacred cow for abortionists? Why does society grant abortionists the privilege to profit from the greatest harm imaginable: dismemberment and poisoning of innocent victims without due process, without anesthesia, and without the right to appeal which even the worst criminals are entitled to?

1. Why is it wrong to rape, but right to kill without being punished?

2. Why is it wrong to sexually abuse little children, but right to execute the unborn without any legal consequence?
3. Why is it wrong to steal and burglarize, but right to ask for the death of innocent unborn children with any legal repercussion?
4. I hope you get the idea!

And why did we back in 1970 allow our church leaders to compromise with this great moral evil by permitting our own hospitals to offer elective abortions on demand which represents a direct violation of our own *"Guidelines on Abortion"* and even what the Lord wrote on tablets of stone with his own finger?

The obvious answer is: Profit! The fear of loss of revenue led our leaders to compromise with evil.

Should we not apologize for this deviation from moral duty? Should we not pray, fast, and seek God's forgiveness for this great sin? The Lord is merciful and ready to forgive![242]

> New International Version
> *if my people, who are called by my name, will humble themselves and pray and seek my face and turn from their wicked ways, then I will hear from heaven, and I will forgive their sin and will heal their land.*

Will There Be Another 9/11?

I have heard people ask whether there will be another 9/11, the dramatic event that took place back on September 11/01, when the Twin Towers of the World Trade Center collapsed following the impact of two airplanes loaded with fuel that had been hijacked by Muslim extremist; a devilish act which dealt a terrible blow to our pride and complacency.

---

[242] 2 Chronicles 7:14.

My immediate reaction to the question: *"Do you think that there might be another 9/11?"* is: *"Yes, of course there will be another 9/11."* Who can prevent a 9/11 from taking place every year in September? Unless, those who are in charge of printing Calendars do agree to skip 9/11, and jump from the tenth of September to the twelfth of the same month.

Isn't this what many hotels do? They do not have a thirteenth floor in their building! You go from the 12th floor to the 14th one, and nobody complains. This would be the easiest way of avoiding another 9/11.

The more difficult way would be to increase the security of our airports, and to augment the domestic and foreign intelligence. Do we deserve to be free from the repetition of the dramatic events that took the life of 3,000 innocent civilians whose only crime was to show up for work on time on 9/11/01? My answer is: *"Yes, aren't we the guardians of democracy and freedom in the world?"*

Our enemies do not agree with me. They accuse us of killing innocent women and children in Iraq and Afghanistan. My answer is: *"We are not targeting women and children in those countries!"*

This is true, nevertheless, we cannot deny the fact that we are targeting our own children here in the U.S. We have slaughtered 56 million of them since the Supreme Court legalized the killing of the unborn.

Given this scenario, do we deserve to be free from another 9/11 tragic event? I am not so sure. In Iraq and Afghanistan, we killed our enemies, with collateral damage to innocent civilians. At home we kill our own. In Afghanistan we killed those who posed a threat to our security. At home we kill those who pose no threat to us. In Iraq we killed those who sponsor terror. At home we slaughter those who are the most innocent and defenseless being in the universe.

Therefore I ask again: What do you think? Will there be another 9/11? Can we rely on God's protection if we continue to slaughter our own children with impunity?

HONORING THOSE WHO DISHONOR GOD

The Signs of Increased Wickedness

 Samuele Bacchiocchi held the position of Professor of Theology at Andrews University at the time of this writing. Back in July 29, 1999, he published a newsletter with the title *"The Signs of Increased Wickedness,"*[243] in which he discussed the effects of the sexual revolution on the American society and the world. Two of the topics he dwelt on the most were homosexuality and abortion. Here are his comments about abortion:

"Perhaps the most tragic consequence of the sexual obsession and permissiveness of our society is the appalling number of unborn babies being aborted in every country of the world. The increase has been facilitated by the legalization of abortion in many countries. In Denmark and Sweden, even minors can have abortions on request-without parental approval.

This incredible suppression of unborn children raises a disturbing question: How can such a thing happen in Christian countries such as the United States? An important answer is to be found in the prostitution of the divine gift of sex: a gift God gave to humanity to procreate and to enable marital partners to become symbolically one by expressing and experiencing total, exclusive, and mutual commitment in self-giving of themselves to one another.

---

[243] Samuele Bacchiocchi, "The Signs of Increased Wickedness" *Endtime Issues* No. 24 (29 July 1999). http://www.biblicalperspectives.com/endtimeissues/eti_24.html

> *How long, one wonders, will God allow this evil to continue? The Scripture reminds us that there is a limit to God's mercy (Gen 15:16). As the Lord brought judgment upon the wicked generations of Noah's and Lot's times, the signs of increasing wickedness just surveyed in this Bible study give us reason to believe that soon He will come again to execute judgment upon the evildoers and to restore order, peace, love, and justice upon this earth."*

I believe that Bacchiocchi was right. God's patience does have a limit. Said limit was reached by the pre-flood generation and by the inhabitants of Sodom and Gomorrah, and our present generation might be very close to said limit. I even wonder sometimes whether the 9/11 tragedy might have been allowed as a warning to what may come in the near future. We should learn a lesson from the people of Nineveh who repented of their evil deeds and thus avoided the destruction of their city.

 As one reads the magnificent way Bacchiocchi describes the ethical morass society has plunged headlong into following the sexual revolution, the strong conviction arises that this man of God must be pro-life, until one stumbles upon the exception he cites as a reasonable justification for abortion: *"There are cases such as incest, rape, or health which may make abortion the only viable solution."*[244]

This exception is actually the main argument of those who defend the pro-choice position. We need to recognize that most of those who defend the pro-choice option are actually against abortion, but they allow certain exceptions such as rape, incest, and the health of the pregnant woman. Once a person allows for those exceptions, he/she has joined the pro-choice/pro-abortion group.

---

[244] Abortion is not the only viable option. Bacchiocchi must have never heard about the adoption alternative!

 This is precisely why the former president of the United States, Bill Clinton, vetoed the partial-birth abortion bill: He insisted that the health of pregnant woman must be allowed as an exception to any pro-life legislation. Of course, if society condones the killing of a baby by puncturing the brain of the fetus minutes before it exits the birth canal because caring for the baby might have a detrimental effect on the mental of physical health of the mother, then we have the door wide open for elective abortions all the way until delivery.

The right of the unborn is sacrificed for the sake of the physical and mental welfare of the mother. In the case of rape and incest, the life of the innocent is crushed while the life of the criminal sexual predator is preserved. For this reason, we need to place Dr. Bacchiocchi among those who did not fully embrace the true pro-life position.

The Sacrament of Abortion

Spectrum published in 2005 an article entitled *"The Sacrament of Abortion,"* [245] authored by Regis Nicoll, in which he makes reference to a book with the same title by feminist and New Age author Ginette Paris, who argued that it is not immoral to choose abortion, because it is a manifestation of pagan morality based on the excuse that by choosing abortion the pregnant woman spares the unborn child a painful destiny.

 This kind of morality is definitely antagonistic to what we find in the Sacred Scriptures of Judaism and Christianity. For those who set aside God's revelation to humanity, the killing of unborn children becomes a religious sacrament akin to the child sacrifices prophets warned the children of Israel to avoid.

Towards the end of his article Nicoll makes the following comment and cites from the Psalms.[246]

---

[245] Fr. Frank Pavone, "The Sacrament of Abortion" *Priests for Life Educational Resources* (n.d.) http://www.priestsforlife.org/columns/columns2002/02-08-12sacramentofabortion.htm
[246] Ps. 139:13

> *"In contrast with those pagan notions, the biblical message is that all of humanity is sacred. Regardless of ethnicity, socioeconomic standing, infirmity, or state of physical or mental development, each person is imprinted with the indelible marks of her Creator. For the Christian, then, the abortion issue boils down to that of personhood."*
>
> *"If life in utero is not human, then no justification for abortion is necessary; if it is human, then no justification is adequate. Perhaps in foreview of this modern dilemma, the Psalmist has provided the needed clarity for a culture infused with the doublethink of Planned Parenthood and neo-paganism: "For you created my inmost being; you knit me together in my mother's womb." ..."*

In Old Testament times, people sacrificed their children in honor of their pagan god Moloch. The victims of this abhorrent practice were burned with fire. Today, we are more sophisticated: we burn them with chemicals, and we do this before they have had a chance to see the light of day. There have been many documented cases of babies who survived a saline abortion. Their skin bore the signs similar to burn victims.

A classic example is that of Gianna Jessen.[247] She survived in spite of the poison injected into her mother's womb, and she bears the marks of the terrible ordeal. She survived because the physician had gone home and the nurse in charge decided to call the ambulance. Had the abortionist been present when she was born alive, he would have finished the task of killing her by strangulation or drowning.

> *"At the emergency room, Gianna was placed in an isolette and given little hope for survival. The attempted abortion left her with cerebral palsy. A foster parent was told that Gianna would never be able to lift her head or arms and could never be anything like "normal." Fortunately, the prognosis was drastically erroneous."*

---

[247] http://www.mccl.org/gianna-jessen-abortion-survivor.html

Abortion defenders would like you to believe that handicapped individuals would be better dead, but the story of Gianna shows that this is not the case. Today she travels extensively around the world and shares her pro-life message of hope.

"Gianna has testified before Congress in support of various pro-life legislative initiatives. Below is an excerpt from her testimony before the Constitution Subcommittee of the House Judiciary Committee on April 22, 1996:"

"I am happy to be alive. I almost died. Every day I thank God for life. I do not consider myself a by-product of conception, a clump of tissue, or any other of the titles given to a child in the womb. I do not consider any person conceived to be any of those things."

Who Is The Antichrist Today?

 The Bible describes the Antichrist as a persecuting power, killing the innocent children of God. In the Middle Ages, the Catholic Church fulfilled this role through its infamous Inquisition. More recently Communist Russia and China persecuted and killed millions of innocent human beings. Likewise, Hitler annihilated six million innocent Jews? The question is: who plays this role today? Who is persecuting and murdering the innocent children of God?

Aren't Christians being persecuted, maimed, and slaughtered today in many Moslem countries? Aren't we Americans murdering a million and a half unborn children every year? Isn't this the nature of the Beast of Revelation? What do predatory beasts do? Don't they target the weak and unprotected? Why is it so difficult for us to discern what is crystal clear? We have wrecked our brains trying to decipher the enigmatic **666** number of the Beast of Revelation, forgetting that we can recognize it by what it does, by its nature and character.

The spirit of Antichrist was originally manifested by Cain, the first murderer in history. Since then, this role was played by different individuals and entities. Pharaoh decreed the murder of all Jewish boys. God miraculously  intervened to save baby Moses from a sure death. Wicked Haman planned the destruction of the Jews, and God intervened again to protect them from extinction. Herod decreed the merciless slaughter of the children in Bethlehem, but God intervened to protect the life of baby Jesus.

If you want to identify the real Antichrist, you need to look at the attitude of those who are persecuting and murdering the innocent children of God today. Are we speaking out against the slaughter of Christians in Africa and other Moslem dominated countries? Are we in the forefront defending those being murdered before they have a chance to take their first breath in our own country?

The Pope is fearlessly wielding its influence in defense of the unborn, while we are arguing that we do not know when human life begins! Who is partaking of the spirit of the Antichrist today? In Germany, we sided with Hitler while the Jews were being exterminated, and now we remain silent in our press while the unborn are being butchered and poisoned. May the Lord have mercy on us!

We strive to Make Man Whole through our medical institutions, but remain silent while innocent babies are being torn to pieces inside the sacred chamber God provided for their protection. We strive to add four or five years to the life of those who had the privilege of being allowed to be born through our stop-smoking programs, while we neglect to join those struggling to protect the unborn. Saving the unborn would add, not four or five years to the life of human beings, but rather eighty or ninety years. Can we see the difference?

Non-Adventists have hundreds of pro-life organizations dedicated to protecting the life of the unborn while we, who have identified ourselves as those who keep God's Commandments, are silent on this life and death issue and have even profited from the abortion genocide. This apathy towards the fate of the unborn must stop. We must repent of this great evil and ask God to forgive us this terrible sin.

Notorious Abortionist is Honored by La Sierra University

 Back in 1964, a young medical student named Edward C. Allred graduated from Loma Linda University and chose to specialize in the profitable business of killing unborn babies whose mothers were faced with unwanted pregnancies. Originally his dream was to become an Adventist evangelist, but for some reason he switched to medicine.

Dr. Allred turned abortion into a very profitable business, and expanded his operation to many California cities. At one point, he owned over twenty abortion clinics in the State and invested some of his incredible earnings into other areas including horse racing.

> *"In 1969, ... [he] founded the "Avalon-Slauson Medical Group," which was later renamed "Family Planning Associates." Although this was before the Supreme Court effectively legalized abortion nationwide in Roe v. Wade (1973), California had already legalized abortion in several situations, and hence many women traveled to California to have abortions."*

Dr. Allred was so successful that by 1980 he *"claimed to have personally aborted a quarter of a million fetuses in the preceding 12 years."*[248] How could a physician perform such an incredible number of abortions in such a short time? His secret was that he reduced the time he spent with a patient to approximately five minutes.[249]

> *"Family Planning Associates expanded to the point where Allred owned 21 abortion clinics in California and two in Chicago. According to a 2001 article in Forbes Magazine, Allred's business generated $70 million in annual gross revenues and $5 million in annual profits."*

---

[248] http://advindicate.com/articles/2560
[249] Ibid.

He became a millionaire, and he did share the financial fruits of his success with some of the educational institutions he had graduated from. One of them was La Sierra University, and this Alma Mater of his decided to honor him by founding the *"Edward C. Allred Center for Financial Literacy and Entrepreneurship."*

 Apparently, LSU saw nothing wrong with accepting money derived from the murder of thousands of innocent unborn unwanted babies. In this, Judas had a higher sense of moral duty, because when he realized that his action facilitated the death of an innocent man, he took the blood money and returned it to those he had received it from. Should not this educational institution do likewise?

Yes, Dr. Allred made an incredible amount of money from his medical practice and from his gambling, but was not free from lawsuits. He was accused of being guilty of a large number of clinical violations, and was the target of lawsuits, but he responded with counter lawsuits, and succeeded because his opponents ran out of money while he had plenty of financial resources.[250]

Is Abortion less Offensive to God than Sabbath Breaking?

Millions have perished in our own land for the crime of being unborn. It is estimated that approximately fifty-six million unborn babies have been either poisoned or butchered by physicians who were trained to save lives, but who, for profit sake, engage in the business of summarily executing those innocent babies waiting to have the rare chance of taking their first breath.

 This is another topic where we, Seventh-day Adventists, have chosen to remain silent while the genocide is taking place. We have plenty of printed space to talk about the importance of worshipping God on the correct day of the week, but we have no interest in raising our voices in condemnation of the slaughter of the innocent babies in our own land. Every weekend, over three

---

[250] http://www.seghea.com/pat/life/newsflash.html

thousand unborn children are sacrificed for the sake of convenience, and those criminal abortionists do this again and again with impunity.

 If we as a nation and as a church continue to remain silent, I believe that the 9/11 event will be followed by other terrible calamities, which will dwarf what happened in New York. God cannot forever remain silent and continue to protect our nation, if we remain silent while those destined to the slaughterhouse go to their death and perish before they have a chance to see the light of day.

This does not surprise me, since historically we have been more concerned about the sacredness of holy time than human life. The same thing happened when Hitler began his genocidal program against the Jews.

We SDAs did turn a blind eye to the plight of the innocent. We were more concerned about making sure Christians were warned about the dangers of worshipping God on the wrong day of the week.

We have championed many good causes. One of them is our concern for the health of those who had the great privilege of being allowed to be born. We have invested our precious resources in our efforts to help those eager to stop smoking, for example.

Why? Because, by doing so, we can add about five years to their life. We are blind to see that, by saving the unborn from a sure death, we could add not merely five years to the life of human beings, but an entire life span.

 We think that by keeping the Sabbath Day Holy, we are rendering a great service to humanity, forgetting that Jesus stated that the Sabbath was made for the sake of man, and not the other way around. We also forget that the Sabbath is a sign, a mere sign. Signs are important.

The sign that reads Emergency in front of a hospital is a big help in guiding ambulances to the place where help is available. Nevertheless, if there is no hospital behind the sign staffed with trained physicians and nurses to render vital help, the sign becomes a dangerous distraction that can cost the life of the dying patient.

 Some time ago, I stopped at the White Estate section of the Loma Linda University library, and checked the list of printed material we have been publishing on the subject connected with the Sabbath. We have spent tons of ink in our efforts to convince the rest of Christians about the need to worship God on the correct day of the week. Then I looked for what we were doing in defense of those being poisoned and butchered inside the womb, the modern torture chamber of humanity.

What did I find? Nothing! Zero! This shows very clearly where our interest is. We proclaim that prenatal human life is a magnificent gift of God which should be protected, and then admit that the church has chosen not to define the precise moment human life begins.[251] I can't understand this! How can we expect our physicians to protect prenatal human life if we affirm that we do not know when human life begins!

 The Pope, whom we have in the past demonized and labeled as the Beast of Revelation knows when human life begins. And yet we, the Remnant church of God don't. Beasts of prey kill the innocent and defenseless. Isn't this what abortionists are doing? Isn't that the true image of the beast? Doesn't this sound like an anomaly to you?

We have labeled the one who is more determined than anybody else in the world to protect the innocent as the Beast. I think that our SDA eyes need to be examined. We have lost our 20/20 vision. How I wish somebody would come to the rescue of those destined to perish.

It is true that in ages past the Catholic Church persecuted, tortured, and killed many Christian, whom Rome labeled as heretics. There is no way of denying what the Catholic Church did through the notorious Inquisition. Nevertheless, should we judge Rome on the basis of what the church did centuries ago, or rather on what the Pope is doing in defense of the

---

[251] Bettina Krause, "ANN Feature: Broader Religious Input Needed in Stem Cell Debate, Says Adventist Ethicist" *Seventh-day Adventist Church/Adventist News network* (7 Aug. 2001). The original online source of the article is no longer accessible, but a copy can be found here: http://remnant-online.com/smf/index.php?topic=5499.0

defenseless today? Should we ignore what Mother Theresa did for the helpless, and what she did for the unborn?

I don't think we should! Credit should be given where credit is due! Shouldn't we join Rome in its tireless effort to protect those who have no legal defense in this land of freedom: Freedom that is restricted for those lucky to have been allowed to be born already? We need to repent of this terrible evil and ask God for forgiveness! His judgments are about to fall on humanity. Let's do this before it is too late!

Nathan Christian's Dilemma

Nathan Christian is not his real name, since he prefers to remain anonymous. He is faced with a moral dilemma resulting from the policies currently followed by the Adventist community of faith since 1970, the year the Adventist Church began to profit from the killing of innocent unborn children.[252]

He was born a Catholic. His mother was a devout religious woman until the last day of her life. Not so his dad, who went to church only on special occasions like weddings and funerals. Nathan became acquainted with the SDA religious beliefs through a neighbor who shared with him some SDA magazines and books.

He especially enjoyed reading a book by Ellen White entitled The *"Desire of Ages"* and *"Steps to Christ."* He is currently reading *"The Great Controversy"* written by the same author and taking Bible studies from the local SDA pastor.

 He is convinced that the correct day for worship is the Seventh Day of the week, as expressed in the Decalogue instead of Sunday. He has managed to attend some of the SDA services on a couple of Sabbaths, but he has been unable to secure all Sabbaths off without risking loosing his job and the nice retirement package that goes with it. He would like to be baptized and thus join the Remnant Church, which keeps *"God's Commandments and has the Testimony of Jesus,"* but he has been told that

---

[252] This story is true to life, but it should be read as an allegory.

working on Sabbaths makes him ineligible for membership in the SDA organization.

Nathan has talked to the management of the company he works for, but so far has been unable to secure Sabbaths off. His immediate supervisor has suggested that he ask his pastor for a dispensation, since working to support his wife and family is a noble task; and, according to him, the pastor should be able to accommodate his special needs. Nathan has tried to reason with the SDA minister in charge of preparing him for baptism to no avail.

 The hardest part for him to understand is based on the fact that Mary, his daughter, who joined the SDA church a few months ago, was allowed to receive the baptismal ritual in spite of the fact that the SDA pastor was aware that she was pregnant and planning to have an abortion, which took place a couple of weeks after her baptism. Nathan cannot understand why violating the Fourth Commandment is considered by the church as a more serious moral offense than taking the life of his grandchild before birth, which is forbidden by another of the Ten Commandments.

He believes that if his daughter got a dispensation to have the abortion, he should be granted likewise a dispensation to work on Sabbaths. Working to support his family seems to be a noble endeavor, especially considering that he has two of his children in a SDA College, and one in a SDA Academy. Loosing his source of income would deprive his children of a religious education, and force him to take a menial job, or perhaps even lose his home to the bank that holds his mortgage.

Nathan can't figure out the logic of the church being so intransigent on the sanctity of Holy Time, while exhibiting laxity when it comes to the Sacredness of Human Life. Do you have any suggestion for this perplexed man?

KEEPING THE BABY WHOLE

"To Make Man Whole" How About Keeping the Unborn Baby Whole?

Loma Linda University, owned and operated by the Seventh-day Adventist Church, proudly displays its motto *To Make Man Whole* in the Loma Linda

 University Medical Center main lobby and in many of its publications, thus declaring the high ideals of service to humanity, and emphasizing the notion that human health encompasses more than physical health, but rather integrates the physical, psychological, and spiritual aspects of our human personality. Healing the body while ignoring the other aspects of our human nature does not provide a solid foundation for physical, mental, and spiritual health.

For many decades Loma Linda University has pursued this high ideal of excellence with remarkable success, and it has graduated thousands of highly

 skilled physician, nurses, and professionals in other medical fields who, following the example of Jesus Christ of Nazareth, have gone to the four corners of the earth carrying with them the lofty ideal of service to a suffering humanity. Its graduates can be found in a large number of countries serving the needs of people with dedication, sacrifice, and Christian love.

How About "To Keep the Baby Whole"?

As I pondered the deep meaning of our Loma Linda University motto "*To Make Man Whole*," I wondered: How about to keep the baby whole? It is true that the university has done a lot, and is providing an outstanding service geared toward those who are waiting to be born; nevertheless, I am rather thinking of what the university, and the church that owns this educational and medical facility, could have done for the unborn in light of the high ideal of service implied in its motto.

What Could the University and the Church Have Done for the Unborn?

 You may wonder what I have in mind! Well, I am thinking of what could have been accomplished on behalf of the unborn, had the university and the SDA Church embraced the pro-life philosophical and humanitarian position instead of the pro-choice/pro-abortion one.

You might be aware that on an average weekend, approximately three thousand innocent unborn babies are either poisoned or dismembered prior to birth by physicians who have been trained in the arts of healing instead of skill in killing.

And this is taking place in some of our SDA hospitals, and even more so inside abortion clinics whose owners' highest aim is profiting from the deaths of these innocent human creatures.

When Does Human Life Begin?

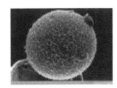 Think about the influence of our Loma Linda University, and the influence of our SDA Church on society. We are known by thousands and millions of people. They are watching and listening to what we are saying about human life

A few years ago, when human cloning and the stem-cell research controversy was in high gear, and Americans were wondering when does human life begin, the SDA Church lost a golden opportunity of siding with the pro-life community by affirming that human life begins at conception.

Instead, the SDA Church issued to the world the incredible declaration that the beginning of human life *"is a moment science finds difficult to pinpoint."*[253]

---

[253] Bettina Krause, "ANN Feature: Broader Religious Input Needed in Stem Cell Debate, Says Adventist Ethicist" *Seventh-day Adventist Church/Adventist News network* (7 Aug. 2001). The original source is no longer accessible online, but you can find a copy here: http://remnant-online.com/smf/index.php?topic=5499.0

The Far Reaching Implications of Our Pro-Choice Position

Such a statement had far-reaching implications, I believe, for the life of untold millions of unborn babies. Notice that while the Roman Pontiff and our Christian Southern Baptists were declaring far and wide that human life begins at conception; we announced to the world that we did not know what the biology books have been publishing for endless decades: that human life begins at conception. The tendency of such a declaration by our church was to strengthen the cause of the pro-abortion community.

Is It True That Our Church is Pro-Choice?

Whenever I bring this subject in my conversation with members of our SDA Church, quite often people are surprised to learn that we are in fact on the Pro-Choice side of this controversy. If you are still in doubt, notice what one of our leaders stated recently:[254]

> *"While I believe with all my heart in freedom, this freedom does not extend to a right to kill an innocent child. To date, my view has not gained the support necessary to commit our church at large to the pro-life cause. James Standish."*

I have in my file similar assertions by several leading Adventists who attempted to convince our church leaders to adopt a pro-life position but failed. One of them told me in a letter that back in 1992, when the church was considering the adoption of the *"Guidelines on Abortion,"* he and others voted for a pro-life position but were outvoted by others.

This led to the adoption of the pro-choice/pro/abortion stance on abortion, and some of our Adventist hospitals began offering abortions on demand in a direct violation of our own guidelines on abortion ant the biblical prohibition against the taking of innocent human life.

---

[254] Comment sent by E-mail from the General Conference of Seventh-day Adventists to a friend of mine.

Our Silence as Additional Evidence of our Moral Support of the Pro-Choice Agenda

If you are still in doubt, I will ask you the following question: When was the last time you heard a sermon, read an article or a book published by our SDA denomination defending the Pro-Life position? A few years ago, I spent a few hours researching in our LLU library in my attempt at locating articles defending the sanctity of human life. I went back about ten years, and I discovered to my amazement that there was almost an absolute silence on the issue, while I had no problem locating hundreds of articles dealing with the Sabbath question.

What is More Sacred, Sacred Time or Human Life?

At this point, I have a question for you: What is more sacred in the eyes of God: Our worship on the correct day of the week, or our respect for innocent human life? You might say: The Sabbath is the most sacred of God's Commandments. Is this really so? How come Jesus did not state that? But he did say in Matthew 25 that our eternal destiny would hinge on the way we treat *"the least of these."* Is there any other group of humans more entitled to belong to such category? Jesus also said:[255]

> *"Let the children come to me! ... I have come that you may have life, and that you may have it more abundantly."*

I ask: How can the children come to him if we either poison or dismember them before they have had a chance to take their first breath? And how can they have an abundant life, if we deprive them of life before they are born? We have been championing the campaign against smoking for many decades now, and thousands of smokers are grateful for what we have done for them. This is very laudable.

---

[255] Matt. 19:14; John 10:10.

By doing this we add four or five years to the life of former smokers. If we did the same for the unborn, we would be adding–not simply four or five years to their life–but rather an entire life span.

More Evidence of Our Moral Support for the Pro-Abortion Cause

But there is additional evidence of our moral support for the Pro-Abortion cause. Notice what John V. Stevens Sr., a former Pacific Union Conference of SDA Adventists Public Affairs/Religious Liberty Director, wrote for the *"Pacific Union Recorder"* on August 20, 1990:

> *"Abortion has become the most controversial and volatile issue in America since the Civil War. . . . That brings us squarely to the ultimate issues–freedom to live and freedom to choose. Does either have a priority? For many the answer comes quickly–the freedom to live. Others would select freedom to choose."*
>
> *"The best example is Christ who chose to die in order to restore that freedom lost through sin so that all can choose to mold their own destiny. Christ values choice over life. . . . From the perspective of respect for God's Word, Biblical history, and the fundamental principle of free moral agency, the Adventist church could justify adopting a pro-choice position. It has not."*

It has not? I'd rather say, *"It has indeed."* All one has to do is carefully read the *"Guidelines on Abortion."*[256] Besides, by affirming that we do not know when human life begins, and by our silence on this issue, I would venture to suggest that we have been strengthening the cause of abortion.

When I read the above-quoted article, I almost fell off my chair. If we can say that Jesus died to restore our freedom to take the life of innocent human beings, then why can't we say the same about adultery, rape, burglary, and Sabbath breaking? Did Christ really die to restore our freedom to fornicate, to murder, rape and dismember or poison the bodies of our own children?

---

[256] http://www.adventist.org/information/official-statements/guidelines/article/go/0/abortion/6/

Read the Old Testament! People had plenty of freedom to sin. We did not lack freedom to sin. Jesus died to free us from sin! This is why Jesus said to the woman caught in adultery: *"Neither do I condemn thee. Go and sin no more."*

Our Undeniable SDA Blind Spot

There is no doubt in my mind that we, SDAs, have developed a blind moral spot and can't see what is crystal clear in the Bible: That shedding innocent

 blood is one of the most abhorrent practices condemned throughout the Bible. Last week I noticed some evidence of this fact as I read the Sabbath School Bible Study Guide (formerly known as the Sabbath Quarterly). In the lesson for Tuesday, February 28, the author, after quoting several Biblical passages describing how some Israelite individuals participated in the pagan ritual of burning their children in honor of God Moloch, he asked the following question:

> *"Though people today don't burn their children on altars to pagan gods, what are some modern parallels to this same practice?"*

The writer answered his own question by saying that a modern counterpart for the burning of children ritual is the way we abuse our children today. My question is: Isn't abortion a better equivalent for the infanticide practiced in Biblical times than child abuse? After reading this, I thought: Evidently we have developed a blind spot in dealing with the abortion issue. We look at the forest, but we can't see the trees!

Two SDA Books Defending the Right to Kill

 Since the abortion controversy started, 41 years ago, I could count only two books published by SDA authors, and both are mainly on the side of women's right to kill the unborn. They are: *What Is a Person*, by James W. Walters; and *Abortion Ethical Issues & Options*, Edited by David R. Larson. The second book is a

221

compilation of presentations made by a large group of SDA leaders, most of them defending women's right to choose.

I have a debt of gratitude towards both of these SDA scholars for their contribution to SDA thinking, but I cannot agree with the Pro-Choice material those books present. Both books illustrate the undeniable fact that the leadership of the SDA Church has a definitely Pro-choice/pro-abortion leaning.

Am I Preaching to the Choir?

Sometime ago, I was talking to one of our church members, and he said: *"I think that you are preaching to the choir!"* Am I? Where is the choir? I ask. If in fact there is a choir supporting my position, then I must say that it is a silent choir that never sings anything. On many occasions people have asked me: Why don't you publish something on the subject? I must confess that I have submitted some of my writings to most of the SDA official and independent publications to no avail.[257]

Some years ago, I submitted a short article to the Adventist Review. I received a message from the assistant editor saying that my submission had been accepted, and there was a check in payment for my contribution. I am still waiting for the magazine to publish what I wrote. At this rate, I will probably be seven feet under by the time they decide to publish it. This is why I started the *SDAForum.Com* , which eventually was replaced by *Advent.life.wordpress.com.*

Have We Learned From the German and Austrian Adventists?

A few years ago the leaders of the German and Austrian SDA Church issued a declaration apologizing for the SDA collaboration and silence during the Nazi extermination program of six million Jews.

---

[257] I must cite two exceptions: One article published by *Adventist Today*, and another one by *Advindicate,* but it took me a decade, a lot of prayers, and a doctoral dissertation to achieve this.

Apologizing is good medicine, but isn't it much better to avoid repeating the same mistake here in America while the genocide of the unborn is taking place? This is my humble opinion!

The Puzzling SDA Apathy Towards the Plight of the Unborn[258]

The Plight of the Unborn

 Never in the history of humankind have the lives of the unborn been at risk on such a mass scale. There is no question but that the womb, the sacred chamber God provided for the protection of the unborn, is today the most dangerous place on earth. According to statistics provided by the *Alan Guttmacher Institute* [Planned Parenthood], the number of abortions performed per year in the U.S. since 1973 averages 1,560,198.[259]

The statistics for the entire world is even scarier: Approximately 46 Million.[260] This surpasses by far any other cause of death, including wars.[261] If car accidents, smoking, or cancer, were responsible for the deaths of such a large number of human beings, I suspect that SDAs would be demanding that something be done to put a stop to such a waste of human life.

Half of all abortions in the U.S. are performed at or before the eight week of pregnancy;[262] which means that approximately 800,000 developing babies are denied the right to life each year at a stage when they look very human, with recognizable arms, legs, head and feet, as revealed by ultrasound pictures.[263]

---

[258] Nic Samojluk. *Adventist Today*, "The Puzzling SDA Apathy Towards the Plight of the Unborn" (Jan/Feb 2007).

[259] "The Consequences of Roe v. Wade" *Central Illinois Right to Life* (n.d.). http://www.cirtl.org/stats.htm

[260] Gregg Cunningham, "Abortion Facts" *The Center for Bio-Ethical Reform* (2003).

[261] John M. Hurt, "Abortion Statistics" *The HTML Bible* (22 Apr. 2004). http://www.htmlbible.com/abortstats.htm

[262] M. Thomas Lothamer, "Gestational Age & Abortion" *Baptists For Life* (n.d.). http://www.bfl.org/Issues-Answers/Abortion/FAQs/Gestational-Age-Abortion.aspx

This is why when an abortion is performed, the nurse must account for all the parts of the dismembered baby to avoid serious health hazards for the mother.

Evidence of Our Apathy

Considering the fact that we claim to be *"God's remnant church on earth"* possessing the *"last message for a perishing world,"* and keeping God's

Commandments,[264] it would be natural to expect that we would be in the forefront of the pro-life movement, because one of those commandments prohibits the taking of human life,[265] and because the Bible contains many similar injunctions prohibiting the *"shedding of innocent blood."*[266] Can an abortion be performed without the shedding of innocent blood?

It must be done before day 21 of pregnancy when most women aren't even aware that they are pregnant! A decade ago I sent a donation to the General Conference and designated the funds as pro-life. The check was returned to me with the following note: *"We do not have a pro-life program in our church."*

Our Puzzling Inconsistency

We have invested a significant amount of time and tons of ink throughout the years in defense of the Sabbath, and we have had an impressive health program that has helped thousands of smokers quit a habit that shortens their lives

by four or five years. Well, Abortion deprives the unborn of their entire life. Have you heard any pro-life sermons lately? How many pro-life articles have you spotted in our SDA publications in the last decade? The message we send to the world is: The Sabbath and extending the life of smokers by four or five years are important. The untimely death of our children before birth is not. A friend of mine sent an E-mail to our local pastor asking why he never

---

[263] Mark Crutcher, "4D Ultrasound Pictures of Unborn Babies" *Pro-Life America.* Com (2006). http://www.prolifeamerica.com/4D-Ultrasound-pictures/
[264] Revelation 12:17.
[265] Exodus 20:13.
[266] Proverbs 6:16, 17; Deuteronomy 19:10.

preached a pro-life sermon. The answer was: *"If I did, some members might get offended."* If that is the case, then why preach at all? Can you imagine John the Baptist, Elijah, Jesus, or Paul saying that?

The Role of Our Guidelines on Abortion

Our official *Guidelines on Abortion*[267] include many lofty pro-life statements such as A. *"Prenatal human life is a magnificent gift of God. God's ideal for human beings affirms the sanctity of human life, in God's image, and requires respect for prenatal life;"* B. *"Abortions for reasons of birth control, gender selection, or convenience are not condoned by the Church;"* C. *"God calls for the protection of human life and holds humanity accountable for its destruction;"* and D. *"God is especially concerned for the protection of the weak, the defenseless, and the oppressed."*

This is great! The problem is that these wonderful pro-life statements are neutralized and negated by others like: A. *"Seventh-day Adventists want to relate to the question of abortion in ways that . . . reflect Christian responsibility and freedom."* B. *"God gives humanity the freedom of choice, even if it leads to abuse and tragic consequences. His unwillingness to coerce human obedience necessitated the sacrifice of His Son."* Does the fact that we have freedom of choice mean that we have a blank check to take the life of the unborn with impunity? I am free to shoot at the president or the pope, but there are serious consequences if I do so.

This emphasis on our freedom of choice, places us as a church on the side of the pro-choice/pro-abortion group. I see in these statements the influence of our religious liberty leaders, which reminds me of one of them named John V. Stevens. On August 20, 1990, The Pacific Union Recorder published an article written by him in which he adamantly defended women's moral right to abortion. His main argument was that Jesus died to give us the freedom of choice and, by submitting to the cross, *"Christ valued choice over life."*

---

[267] Seventh-day Adventist Church. Adventist Beliefs/Guidelines: *Guidelines on Abortion* (12 Oct. 1992). http://www.adventist.org/information/official-statements/guidelines/article/go/0/abortion/6/

If that is the case, then perhaps Jesus also died to give rapists, burglars, child abusers, terrorists and murderers their freedom of choice! Contrast these statements with what James White published about abortion:[268]

Some argue that Ellen White never wrote about abortion. After reading what her husband wrote, do you think she needed to add anything else? The defenders of abortion also argue that the Bible is rather silent on abortion. Well, I have news for them: The Bible is also silent about slavery, genocide, and polygamy. Am I morally free to enslave others or have several wives?

The *Guidelines on Abortion* call for the *"protection of human life,"* but *"the church has chosen not to define the precise moment human life begins."*[269] Science does know when human life begins,[270] and other church organizations and political groups do know this as well; but we, the *"Remnant Church of God"* have chosen to ignore this! I ask: What good can calling for the protection of human life be if we have decided to ignore when said life begins?

The Question of Personhood

Back in 1973, nine unelected justices of the U.S. Supreme Court deprived the unborn of personhood, thus making the way clear for the merciless killing of the unborn; and more recently, a renowned and highly esteemed Loma Linda University professor[271] published a book with the title *What is a Person,* questioning the personhood of the unborn. What does the Bible say about the personhood of the unborn? In Isaiah 49:1 we find the following statement: *"The Lord called me from the womb."* How can God call a non-person to be his prophet? We have a similar statement regarding another major prophet:[272]

---

[268] James White. *Solemn Appeal* (Battle Creek, Michigan: Stem Press, 1870), 100.
[269] Bettina Krause, "ANN Feature: Broader Religious Input Needed in Stem Cell Debate, Says Adventist Ethicist" *Seventh-day Adventist Church/Adventist News network* (7 Aug. 2001). This article is no longer accessible online from the original source but there is a copy here of the document: http://remnant-online.com/smf/index.php?topic=5499.0
[270] "The Case Against Abortion: Medical Testimony" *Abort 73.Com* (n.d.). http://www.abort73.com/abortion/medical_testimony/
[271] James W. Walters.
[272] Jeremiah 1:5.

> *"Before I formed you in the womb I knew you, and before you were born I consecrated you; I have appointed you a prophet to the nations."*

And regarding John the Baptist, the inspired evangelist Luke said: *"He will be filled with the Holy Spirit, while yet in his mother's womb."*[273] Is this applicable to a non-person? A similar statement is made by Paul: *"But when He who had set me apart, even from my mother's womb . . ."*[274] Does the Lord consecrate non-persons as his representatives on earth?

 History has shown that the deprivation of personhood on a selective basis has been practiced since the dawn of civilization. For many centuries women, slaves, and members of specific ethnic groups have been legally stripped of personhood and subjected to abuse, torture, and even death.[275]

The first step towards the enslavement or extermination of certain groups of human beings has been to deprive them of personhood. It took a civil war to restore the personhood of the American slaves, and a world war to restore the right to life of Jews. Do we need another civil war to restore the unborn rights to life? The defenders of abortion emphasize women's right to freedom. How about the unborn's right to freedom from unjust execution?

Are We Repeating History?

 By looking the other way while millions of unborn are deprived of life we are repeating history. Recently, the German and Austrian SDA leaders issued a public apology for our cooperation with the Hitler Nazi regime while the slaughter of the Jews was taking place. Unless we alter our indifference towards the unborn, I will venture to predict that we are doomed to apologize

---

[273] 1:15.
[274] Galatians 1:15.
[275] Keith L. Moore, "Making a Person Property" *Abort 73.Com* (2005).

again at some time in the future for our apathy towards the plight of the unborn.

My Response to Jim Walters.[276]

In his critique of my article, Jim Walters included some new issues and a couple of non-issues. The *"Flat View of Human Life"* and the threat to the life of the pregnant woman are non-issues. I have never equated the value of a single-celled entity with the moral value of an adult. There is a huge moral difference between shooting at the president and attempting to assassinate a burglar. The law distinguishes between first-degree and a second-degree murder. Manslaughter is not morally equivalent to murder. Nevertheless the killing of an innocent beggar or a non productive member of the human race is still murder.

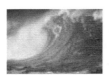 It is true that nature does kill with spontaneous abortions and floods, tornados, tsunamis and earthquakes; while humans who imitate nature quite often end in jail or the electric chair. The Bible is silent on abortion; but it fails to condemn slavery, polygamy, and genocide as well; which means that the argument from silence is inappropriate. God allows for personal freedom, but there are serious consequences for misusing it. If we allow abortion on the basis of freedom, then why not allowing rape, stealing, and child abuse as well?

 The image of God is more than *"the power to think and to do."* It includes the power to do God's will, and his will is that we "choose life" for the unborn! *"God is love,"* and this love prompted him to grant the human race a second chance. Abortion denies the unborn even the first chance on life, and punishes the innocent for the crimes or mistakes of others, which cannot be equated with a lesser evil. Nine months of inconvenience can never compensate for the total deprivation of life.

---

[276] In the same issue of *Adventist Today* the editor did include Jim Walters' critique of my article, and this represents my response to said critique.

God's Message to the U.S. and Adventism

The Lord has a message for the leaders of both the U.S. and the Adventist Church, and it is: Repent. The mass genocide of the unborn must stop! We cannot deny the right to life to a large segment of the human race with impunity.

If we continue to ignore God's demands enshrined in his Law, the incredible blessing we received from his generous hand will become a terrible curse and we will perish like King Pharaoh of Egypt and like Hitler.

The Lord needs your help in spreading this warning far and wide before God's patience runs thin and his judgments begin to fall without mercy on his chosen nation and his chosen people. Unless we repent, the 9/11 event will be repeated in a much larger scale.

Heaven will not wait forever! We are on the verge of moving past the point of no return. The inhabitants of Nineveh repented in ashes and sackcloth, and God saved them from destruction. The Noah generation did not, and swift punishment followed. We need to learn from history!

New International Version
"This day I call the heavens and the earth as witnesses against you that I have set before you life and death, blessings and curses. Now choose life, so that you and your children may live" [Deut. 30:19]

IF YOU WILL NOT READ THIS BOOK AGAIN, DO NOT LET IT GATHER DUST—GIVE IT TO SOMEBODY ELSE! LET THE BOOK FULFILL ITS SACRED MISSION!